MANJEET MANN

Manjeet is an actress, author, playwright and screenwriter. *Run, Rebel* is her debut YA novel. It was shortlisted for the Carnegie Medal in 2021 and won the Carnegie Shadower's Choice Award, Diverse Book Award, UKLA Book Award and Sheffield Children's Book Award YA category. It was one of *The Scotsman*'s Best Books for Teens and a *Guardian* Best Book of 2020. Her second YA novel, *The Crossing,* won the Costa Children's Book Award and was the overall winner of the Sheffield Children's Book Award 2022. It was also shortlisted for the Carnegie Medal in 2022, the Waterstones Book Prize and YA Book Award, as well as being a *Sunday Times* Book of the Week.

Manjeet is also the founder of Run The World, a not-for-profit working with women and girls from marginalised backgrounds and using sport and theatre as a means to empower and train future community leaders.

Manjeet Mann

RUN, REBEL

adapted from the novel by Manjeet Mann

NICK HERN BOOKS

London
www.nickhernbooks.co.uk

A Nick Hern Book

Run, Rebel first published in Great Britain as a paperback original in 2023 by Nick Hern Books Limited, The Glasshouse, 49a Goldhawk Road, London W12 8QP, in association with Pilot Theatre

Run, Rebel (book) copyright © 2020 Manjeet Mann, published by Penguin Books

Run, Rebel (play) copyright © 2023 Manjeet Mann

Manjeet Mann has asserted her right to be identified as the author of this work

Cover illustration: Manjit Thapp

Designed and typeset by Nick Hern Books, London
Printed in Great Britain by Mimeo Ltd, Huntingdon, Cambridgeshire PE29 6XX

A CIP catalogue record for this book is available from the British Library

ISBN 978 1 83904 221 8

Woodland
CARBON
www.woodlandcarbon.co.uk
NICK HERN BOOKS
Printed on Carbon Captured paper

Contents

Run, Rebel was first performed at Mercury Theatre, Colchester on 25 February 2023, before touring to York Theatre Royal; Derby Theatre; Belgrade Theatre, Coventry and Alnwick Playhouse. The cast and creative team was a follows:

AMBER	Jessica Kaur
HARBANS/ENSEMBLE	Pushpinder Chani
SURINDER/ENSEMBLE	Asha Kingsley
RUBY, BEENA/ENSEMBLE	Simran Kular
TARA/ENSEMBLE	Hannah Millward
DAVID/ENSEMBLE	Kiran Raywilliams
Writer	Manjeet Mann
Director	Tessa Walker
Designer	Debbie Duru
Lighting Designer	Ben Cowens
Video Designer	Daniel Denton
Associate Video Designer	Ben Glover
Sound Designer	Yvonne Gilbert
Composer	Niraj Chag
Movement Director	Kuldip Singh-Barmi
Associate Movement Director	Ayesha Fazal
Casting Director	Olivia Barr
Casting Consultant	Polly Jerrold Casting
Casting Associate	Francesca Tennant
Staff Director	Neetu Singh

FOR PILOT THEATRE

Tour Production Manager	Luke James
Company Stage Manager	Emily Walls
Deputy Stage Manager	Jeanette Maggs
Assistant Stage Manager	Lizzie Hayward
National Press and PR	Clíona Roberts
Rehearsal and Production Photography	Pamela Raith

Artistic Director and Joint Chief Executive	Esther Richardson
Executive Producer and Joint Chief Executive	Amanda Smith
Company Administrator	Sarah Rorke
Marketing and Projects Producer	Lucy Hammond
Creative Associate	Oliver O'Shea
Digital Officer	Sam Johnson
Finance Director	Helen Nakhwal
Livestreaming and Development	Melanie Paris
Comms and Admin Officer	Lucy Havelock
Education Consultant	Carolyn Bradley

FOR MERCURY THEATRE

Producer	Jenny Moore
Production Manager	Richard Parr
Company Stage Manager	Rebecca Samuels
Head of Construction	Phil Attwater
Workshop Deputy	Harriet Bonner
Workshop Assistant	Jim Bonner
Freelance Workshop	Robert van der Parker
Scenic Artist	David Thomas
Scenic Artist	Rhiannan Howell
Costume Supervisor	Chantelle Regan
Wardrobe Manager	Corinna Vincent
Technical Manager	Emily Holdmen Kingsman
Lighting Programmer	Alex Ray
Production Sound	Wesley Laing Sam Copus
Production Video	Orion Nichol
Production Lighting	Hazuki Mogan
Marketing	Molly Richardson
Schools' Producer	Forest Morgan

Characters

AMBER, *fifteen years old*
HARBANS, *Amber's dad, late forties*
SURINDER, *Amber's mum, early forties*
RUBY, *Amber's sister, early twenties*
DAVID, *Amber's friend, fifteen years old*
TARA, *Amber's friend, fifteen years old*
BEENA, *David's mum, thirty-one*

Other characters
MISS SUTTON, TEACHERS, GEMMA, STUDENTS, JOB
CENTRE WORKER, NEIGHBOURS, MCDONALD'S
WORKER

Note on the Text

Any speech in this font refers to a different moment in time.

All characters other than Amber double/multi-role.

The company are on stage throughout.

Note on the Dialogue

A dash (–) at the end of a line indicates an interruption from
the next speaker.

A slash (/) at the end of a line indicates overlapping dialogue.

*This text went to press before the end of rehearsals and so may
differ slightly from the play as performed.*

ACT ONE

AMBER. We all have a story to tell.
　　Every one of us.

　　She points to members of the audience.

　　You have a story.
　　You have a story.
　　I bet you have a story.
　　I can tell you have a story.
　　You have a story, you have a story...
　　Every. Single. One of us has a story to tell.
　　And we should be allowed to tell it right?
　　We should take control of it,
　　we should own it.
　　It's the only way to be truly free.

　　I'm Amber. I'm fifteen and I live here,
　　Palm Wood Estate.
　　One of the roughest and biggest estates in the country.
　　Streets-in-the-sky dreams
　　turned to sinkhole nightmares.
　　A bunch of concrete towers,
　　looming over you.
　　Windows like Mona Lisa eyes,
　　watching you, following you, there's no hiding...

　　I live in that house,
　　with my mum and dad.
　　I've got an older sister, Ruby,
　　but she doesn't live with us any more.

　　So, this is it.
　　My story.
　　I've waited a long time to tell it.

All the secrets I've been holding inside
about dreams so big.
A love so grand,
a life half lived.
About Mum, about Ruby, about Dad, about me.
How we fought.
How we survived.
How we ran.
How we rebelled.
How we broke free.

First day back at school.

She runs.

Past the bookie's,
the chippy,
the newsagent's.
Dodge the dog shit,
down a dirty alley,
past the garage,
till I get to...

AMBER *stops.*

St Martin's Church!
My sanctuary.
Open skies
away from prying eyes.

TARA *and* DAVID *enter.*

Here they are,
my bezzy mates.
Tara and David.
They say three's a crowd
but not with us.

TARA. AmberAmberAmber! I've missed your beautiful face!

AMBER *(to audience).* Tara's the only person that ever calls me
    beautiful.

DAVID. Sister from another mister, come here!

AMBER. Brother from another mother!

They playfight and then hug.

(*To audience.*) Holy hell. He's er… changed over the summer.

AMBER *takes a deep breath in as they embrace.*

(*To audience.*) Mmmm strawberry chewing gum and Lynx.

Would you mind if we did that again? Thanks.

DAVID. Sister from another mister, come here!

AMBER. Brother from another mother!

She smells his breath.

(*To audience.*) Oh god, sooo good!

One more time. Please.

DAVID. Sister from another mister, come here!

AMBER. Brother from another mother!

She sniffs his chest.

(*To audience.*) He smells sooooo goooood!!!!

AMBER *hugs* DAVID *for a little longer than she should.*

Fine… Okay I admit it. I love him. I do. I really do. Ever since Year 7. I mean come on… look at him… Eyes. Hair. Cheekbones. Arms. Has he been lifting weights? Hel-lo. Legs… Chest. Looks like he's about to pop out of his shirt and let's not forget that mouth. Mouth. Mouth. Mouth…

TARA. You alright, Amber?

AMBER. Yeah, totally fine. Never better…

TARA. You're acting weird.

AMBER. I'm not.

(*To audience.*) Shit.

TARA *begins cleansing* AMBER*'s aura.*

What are you doing?

TARA. Cleansing your aura, your energy is a bit wonky.

AMBER. Would you… please… stop, my energy is fine.

DAVID. Best to let her get on with it. She's been doing cleansing rituals and energy healing on me all summer.

AMBER (*to the audience*). Whoa whoa whoa, stop the action for a sec. What the frig has been going on here?

She collects herself.

What do you mean?

DAVID. It's not a big deal.

TARA. Not a big deal?! We went on holiday, it was the best! /

DAVID. We missed you /

TARA. The weather was amazing! /

DAVID. Wished you were there… /

TARA. We went DIVING, Amber! DIVING!

AMBER (*to audience*). I'm gonna puke. /

DAVID. It really wasn't that big of a deal. /

TARA. Are you kidding? We swam with dolphins! /

AMBER (*to audience*). I'm literally gonna do a stress puke.

DAVID. Yeah but… /

TARA. It was the best holiday ever!

DAVID. Would have been even better if you were there. /

TARA. Oh charming thanks… /

DAVID. No, you know what I mean, we both said it felt like something was missing.

TARA. Yeah that's right. You did say that. I bought you something…

TARA *rummages in her bag.*

DAVID (*whispering to* AMBER). Sorry I didn't tell you. Our mums just booked it.

AMBER. It's fine, honestly. What she got me?

DAVID. Something to help with your… emotions /

AMBER. Emotions? /

DAVID. You know… stress… home /

AMBER. What does she know about my home?… /

DAVID. Nothing… /

TARA. Found it! Open it.

AMBER *opens the gift*.

AMBER. A candle. Thanks.

TARA. A *sage* candle. It'll help cleanse any negative energy by balancing out your chakras. You should light it when you meditate…

AMBER *and* DAVID *share a look*.

I saw that look! It works, okay. My mum cleanses the energy in our house with a sage stick every week and…

DAVID. And what? /

TARA. I'm not telling you /

AMBER. Go on… /

TARA. You're just gonna make fun /

DAVID/AMBER. We're not /

TARA. And… it makes you feel more connected to mother earth /

AMBER. It's great…

AMBER *playfully wafts it around the space*.

I feel cleansed already.

TARA. Give it back if you're just gonna make fun.

AMBER. No, I'm sorry. I love it.

TARA. Whatever. How was your summer break anyway, Ambs?

AMBER. Erm… Fine. Nothing to report really.

(*To audience*.) Just a regular boring summer break.

A buzzing, like electricity along with pulsing of lights.

SURINDER. It wasn't your fault.

DAVID. You okay, Amber?

AMBER. Yeah.

TARA. Where'd you go?

AMBER. Nowhere, I'm fine.

AMBER *looks at the audience.*

(*To audience*.) School.
A place to be my-self
not half-self,
self-loving-self
vibrant-self
fun-self
thriving-self
my
true-self.

A chorus of students surround DAVID *in a classroom like a pack of wild animals.*

AMBER *and* TARA *sit next to him just watching all the other students fawning over him.*

STUDENT 1. Hey David.

STUDENT 2. Hey David.

GEMMA. Hey David.

STUDENT 1. Hey David.

STUDENT 2. Hey David.

GEMMA. Hey David.

DAVID. Hi.

GEMMA. Loving your highlights.

DAVID. Thanks, it's natural. Just happens in the sun.

GEMMA. Looks cute.

AMBER. Girls.

TARA. Boys.

AMBER. Giggling.

TARA. Staring.

AMBER. Flirting.

TARA. Twirling.

STUDENT 1. Hey David.

STUDENT 2. Hey David.

GEMMA. Hey David. Did you have a nice summer?

DAVID. Er yeah.

GEMMA. You been working out?

DAVID. Er…

GEMMA. We should hang out.

DAVID. Er…

The students disperse as quickly as they came and settle at their desks.

TARA. Such weird energy today /

AMBER. Can you believe Gemma /

TARA. I knew I should've brought my crystals with me /

AMBER. She's blatantly flirting /

TARA. I know. /

AMBER stares at GEMMA.

AMBER. She's got some nerve.

(*To audience*.) School field.

Muddy, damp, cold.
I love it. I'm on my own,
I get transported,
I feel free.
It's the only time I ever really feel FREE...
Hockey at our school is like gang warfare
an hour of getting battered and bruised
girls coming at you with sticks
aiming for ankles,
but the running track...

The track is my time.
No matter how small or quiet
I'm expected to be at home,
I find my voice on the running track
It's where I'm truly alive.
Words boomerang from trainer to tarmac,
creating ripples in every corner of my body
until all knock-downs, run-ins, face-offs and scraps
have been twisted, wrung, exhausted and
released up, up, up,
into the clouds and sky above.

I shift my thoughts
try and make sense of stuff
and come out the other side newer, happier, better.
ALWAYS better than before.
It feels like the world slows down.
Allowing me to catch up with thoughts that usually race.
I go to places in my head that aren't here,
of this place,
of this time.
The lines in my head get tangled see
running makes the lines straighter
turns down the rage in my stomach
loosens the phantom grip on my throat.
Running gives me a purpose.

Running,
gives me a reason to live.

Focus. Inhale. Exhale.

MISS SUTTON. Go.

AMBER *runs*.

AMBER (*to audience*). Legs rotating
Trainers striking tarmac.
Quick breaths,
Sharp looks
To my left, Sarah, behind for now.
To my right, Leanne, neck and neck.
Heart pumping,
Legs pounding,
Arms propelling.
Flashes of that night.
The crying.

She stumbles. Lights flicker. Lines blur.

HARBANS. I said no to the running team. It's time she started thinking about marriage. /

SURINDER. That can wait. She's really good, best in her school. /

AMBER (*to audience*). Smashed plates.

HARBANS. She's not a little girl any more. People will talk. /

SURINDER. But her teacher thinks. /

HARBANS. I said no!

AMBER (*to audience*). The blood.

A loud buzz. Lights continue to flicker.

Lines blur.

MISS SUTTON. Keep it tight, Amber, stay in your lane!

AMBER. Just the spark I need.
Waves of electricity firing through…
Arms

Legs
Heart
Veins…
As I cross the finish line, first!

MISS SUTTON. You're still our star runner, Amber!

AMBER. Thanks, miss.

MISS SUTTON. You're still drifting out of your lane as you come through the curve. You have to keep your arms tight to your body and your eyes straight down the track. Your right arm's swinging out and it's kicking you out of your lane.

AMBER. I know, miss, sorry.

MISS SUTTON. See you Tuesday, for training?

AMBER. Erm… I can't compete this year, miss.

MISS SUTTON. What? Why?

AMBER. I've got to focus on other stuff.

MISS SUTTON. It's never interfered with anything before.

AMBER. Can't, miss.

MISS SUTTON. What about the ESACs, Amber? You've got a shot at being on the British team.

AMBER. I just… I can't, miss.

MISS SUTTON. I thought this was what you wanted. /

AMBER. It is. /

MISS SUTTON. I don't understand. /

AMBER. It's not up to me. /

MISS SUTTON. Then who?

AMBER. My dad.

MISS SUTTON. Why?

AMBER. Just his way, miss.

MISS SUTTON. But this is your future.

Silence.

Why don't we set up a meeting, I could talk to him. /

AMBER. It won't help, miss.

MISS SUTTON. Maybe a letter home? Explaining you're our star runner. /

AMBER. Won't help either.

MISS SUTTON. You can't give up.

AMBER (*to audience*). That's the problem with privilege. If you have it, it can be hard to imagine why others can't live as freely as you.

(*To* MISS SUTTON.) Give up? You really think I want to give up?

MISS SUTTON. No. I don't think you do.

AMBER. Can we just stop talking about it?

MISS SUTTON. You know there's only one other athlete I've taught who's shown the same talent as you… I see the same spark in you as I saw in her. You both come alive on the track.

AMBER. Sorry, miss.

MISS SUTTON. No need to be sorry. I just want you on the team.

Leave it with me. I'll see what I can do.

AMBER *takes off her trainers. The sole is hanging off one trainer.*

We might have some in lost property if that helps.

AMBER. It's fine.

MISS SUTTON. If you don't mind, I will write that letter for you.

AMBER. If you like. But I'm telling you, it won't help.

MISS SUTTON *exits.* AMBER *looks at her trainer. She takes some superglue out of her bag. She squeezes it around the sole of her trainer and holds it together.*

ESACs – English Schools Athletics Championships.

First-inter-school games
you win
you make it to regional finals
you win
you compete at county level.
you win
you're on track to making TEAM GB!

AMBER *takes a moment to dream.*

I can't take Miss Sutton
Looking all kinds of hopeful.
Like comparing me to Olympic athlete Allie Reid
is all it'll take
to reverse decisions
out of my control.
Miss Sutton coached her
she always says…
'I see the same spark in you as I saw in her.
You both come alive on the track.'

HARBANS. I said no.

SURINDER. It's just a school team.

HARBANS. I'm warning you, don't even think about going behind my back?

SURINDER (*to* AMBER). It wasn't your fault.

AMBER (*to audience*). But it was my fault.
No more running
No more training sessions with David.
No. More. Dreaming.

TARA *enters.*

TARA. Is that true? You're not gonna be on the team this year?

AMBER. Yeah.

TARA. But what about the ESACs?

AMBER. It's not a big deal.

TARA. Not a big deal? You nearly won last year.

AMBER. Just drop it. Please.

TARA. Do you want to talk about it?

AMBER. No.

TARA. Okay.

Silence.

Do you want to see some holiday pics?

AMBER. Yeah, why not.

TARA. These are the ones of us diving. Have you ever been?

AMBER. No.

TARA. Oh my god, you have to try it. It was amazing. We saw an octopus! It was just magical, honestly, I've never seen anything like it. It's another world. This is when we went paragliding, look at us holding hands, turns out David's scared of heights, can you believe it? Did you know? /

AMBER. No. /

TARA. He was holding my hand so tight. It was so funny. This is when a bird shat on David's shoulder, hilarious, look at his face… and oh my god… this was actually the best… we went on an epic sunset walk, watching sunset on a beach is beautiful, isn't it. /

AMBER. I wouldn't know. /

TARA. Well, it is and we lit these lanterns and they just floated off into the sky, we watched them as we walked barefoot through the sand. It was out of this world…

AMBER *(to audience)*. My brain feels like it's going to explode.

STUDENT 2. Did they kiss?

STUDENT 3. Are they in love?

STUDENT 4. Is three a crowd?

AMBER. Did they talk about me?

STUDENT 1. Three's a crowd, right?

AMBER. If they did talk about me, what did they say?

STUDENT 2. Do they still want to be mates?

AMBER. Do they want me out of the group?

STUDENT 3. He can't love her. He can't.

STUDENT 4. He can love her. He can.

STUDENT 1. Look at her, she's beautiful. There's no contest.

AMBER. She's my friend. Stop thinking of it as a contest.

STUDENT 2. Then why so bothered?

TARA. This is us playing mini-golf in the Bull Ring. /

AMBER. So did you two hang out all summer? /

TARA. Yeah, a bit, I mean, not lots. /

AMBER (*to audience*). How much is A BIT?

STUDENT 3. What does she mean, NOT LOTS?

STUDENT 4. Every week?

STUDENT 1. Every day?

STUDENT 2. Every other day?

AMBER (*to audience*). What is the measure of time between A BIT and NOT LOTS?!

TARA. Are you okay? Sorry we didn't ask you, it's just… We knew you wouldn't be allowed.

AMBER (*spiky*). It's fine.

GEMMA *starts singing*.

Wish she'd shut her face.

TARA. Ignore her.

AMBER. It's hard when someone's that annoying.

(*Loudly.*) Someone needs to call the RSPCA, a cat's being strangled.

GEMMA *stops singing*.

TARA. You know it takes way more energy to be angry than it does to be happy?

AMBER. What you on about?

TARA. You're actually giving her more of your time and headspace hating on her. She's not worth it.

AMBER. She's just so… *look at me, I'm so popular and pretty, I can talk crap about anyone I like and get away with it…*

TARA. You fancy coming to Maccy D's with me and David?

AMBER. I dunno. /

TARA. Oh just come. It'll be fun. We never get to hang out.

AMBER. Alright then.

GEMMA *walks towards them,* AMBER *steps in front of her blocking her path.* GEMMA *steps one way,* AMBER *blocks her, she steps another way,* AMBER *blocks her path. They stare at each other,* AMBER *trying to intimidate, finally letting her pass.*

Scene changes to town centre. It's as though every passer-by is staring at AMBER. TARA *and* DAVID *mess around.* AMBER *is anxious.*

(*to audience*). On our way to Maccy-D's.
My mind's elsewhere.
Concentrating on not being seen.
Looking out for familiar faces
Avoiding well-known places
Where aunties and uncles might work or shop.
'Is she where she should be?'
'Should she be out this late?'
'Who is that she's walking with?'

DAVID. What's this about you not being on the team this year.

AMBER. You know what my dad's like.

DAVID. Yeah but surely he'd be proud?

AMBER. Yeah, if he was a normal dad, I'm sure he would be. We can't all be blessed with mums like yours.

DAVID. You should let Miss Sutton write that letter.

AMBER. A letter's not gonna make any difference.

TARA. But when he reads it. /

AMBER. He won't read it, Tara. /

DAVID. But running's your... *thing...*

AMBER. I know.

DAVID. So sod him, just do it anyway. I need you. Dynamic training duo and all that.

AMBER. Ha! If only it was that easy. Can we just drop it? Please.

DAVID. Who's gonna be my training partner now?

AMBER. I'm sure you won't have trouble finding one.

They stop at traffic lights.

David, don't stand next to me.

DAVID. Where else am I supposed to stand?

TARA *and* DAVID *continue a conversation under* AMBER*'s address to the audience.*

AMBER (*to audience*). Legs feeling weak.
Heart thumping.
Stomach churning.
Throat choking.

I'm so panicked I don't register *her*.
Her coming out of Wilko's
an auntie double-taking me,

eyeballing me from across the road and watching,
watching me walking with Tara and David.
I don't see her till it's too late.

(*To* TARA *and* DAVID.) Shit. That woman saw me!

TARA. I don't think she did, mate.

DAVID. She didn't, Amber.

TARA. I think you're being paranoid.

AMBER (*to audience*). McDonald's.

MCDONALD'S WORKER. Next.

AMBER *steps forward*.

AMBER. Cheeseburger please.

MCDONALD'S WORKER. Your dad's gonna go mad.

AMBER. What?

MCDONALD'S WORKER. Do you want fries with that?

AMBER. Er… yeah, sure.

MCDONALD'S WORKER. You've got twenty minutes max,
pass your lateness off as a meeting with a teacher.

AMBER. Excuse me?

MCDONALD'S WORKER. If you go for the meal deal you get
a drink for free.

AMBER. I've got to go.

DAVID. Come on stay a bit longer.

AMBER. You know I can't.

DAVID. Just five minutes.

AMBER. I wish I could.

TARA. Do you want me to cleanse your aura before you go?

AMBER. No, Tara, I think I'll be fine.

You two have fun.

MCDONALD'S WORKER. Backstabbing bitch. She totally
    wants him.

AMBER. What?

MCDONALD'S WORKER. Have a nice day.

Scene change.

AMBER. Take the backstreets
    Sprint down a dirty alley,
    Round the back of the bus garage
    Sprint past the park.
    Up the hill,
    Turn onto the estate…
    Thighs burning all the way up to the front door.
    Sweaty and smiling.
    Nothing to worry about.
    Endorphins helping me forget.
    Got me seeing through rose-tinted glasses.

    (*To audience.*) It's fine.

    (*To self.*) It's fine.

    (*To audience.*) Endorphins still playing their tricks.

    AMBER*'s home –* HARBANS *is slightly drunk.*

HARBANS (*in Punjabi*). Where were you?

AMBER (*in Punjabi*). School. /

HARBANS (*in Punjabi*). You're lying. /

AMBER (*in Punjabi*). I'm not lying. /

HARBANS (*in Punjabi*). What were you doing at *school*? /

AMBER (*in Punjabi*). I was talking to a teacher… /

HARBANS (*Punjabi*). What teacher?

    Where did you learn to lie like this? /

AMBER (*in Punjabi*). I'm not. /

HARBANS (*in Punjabi*). Your mother? Your mother teach you
    to lie like this? /

AMBER (*in Punjabi*). No. /

AMBER *tries to go*.

HARBANS (*in Punjabi*). Where do you think you're going? I'm not finished. /

AMBER (*in Punjabi*). I've got homework to do. /

HARBANS (*in Punjabi*). I said I'm not finished. Hey… I'm talking to you…

I know you were in town… /

AMBER *stops the action*.

AMBER (*to audience*). Language.
The basis of communication right?
So, how do I communicate
my story
if most of you
can't understand the language?
In this story –
My story
My parents can't speak English
Most of you
I'm guessing
Can't speak Punjabi.
So let's speak English then.
And when
me, Mum and Dad
are speaking to each other
just imagine we're telling you, the audience
our story
in Punjabi.

HARBANS. Where were you?

AMBER. School. /

HARBANS. You're lying. /

AMBER. I'm not lying. /

HARBANS. What were you doing at *school*? /

AMBER. I was talking to a teacher... /

HARBANS. What teacher?

Where did you learn to lie like this? /

AMBER. I'm not. /

HARBANS. Your mother? Your mother teach you to lie like this? /

AMBER. No. /

AMBER *tries to go*.

HARBANS. Where do you think you're going? I'm not finished...

AMBER. I've got homework to do. /

HARBANS. I said I'm not finished. Hey... I'm talking to you...

I know you were in town. You were seen with that woman's son from the community centre. That woman who has zero respect for anyone.

THE MAN *comes out of his house. He tends to his rose bush.* AMBER *stands. She looks at him.*

Do I need to remind you of The Man across the road.
The Man who killed his daughter –
The daughter who shamed the family –
The family
The community
who keep quiet –
Quiet when I give the instruction –
The instruction that will see you disappear –
Disappear like his daughter.

It would just take one phone call.
I can read the lies in your eyes.

HARBANS *leaves*.

AMBER *(to audience)*. Legs. Heavy.
Head. Light.

Stomach. Sick.
Breath. Quick.
Quick. Quicker.
No. Oxygen.
No. Breath.
No. Breath. No breath…

AMBER *is stood frozen*.

DAVID and BEENA*'s home*.

BEENA. Where you been?

DAVID. Went to Maccy D's.

BEENA. You'll ruin your appetite. I'm making your fave.

DAVID. Indian-style shepherd's pie?

BEENA. Yep. How spicy do you want it?

DAVID. Er, mild.

BEENA. Mild? Just like your dad. A couple of lightweights the pair of you…

DAVID. He made a proper spicy chicken last weekend.

BEENA. I stand corrected. (*Beat*.) How was school?

DAVID. Alright. (*Beat*.) Mum?

BEENA. What?

DAVID. Nothing. Forget it.

BEENA. You okay?

DAVID. Yeah… No, not really.

BEENA. What's up?

DAVID. I mean, it's not me, I'm fine.

BEENA. Then who? Jesus, David, spit it out.

DAVID. It's Amber. I'm worried about her. Her dad won't
let her join the running team this year…I think something
happened over the summer. /

BEENA. Like what?

DAVID. Dunno. She's acting weird. /

BEENA. What do you mean?

DAVID. Like she's hiding something.

BEENA. Do you want me to talk to her?

DAVID. Would you?

BEENA. Might be a good idea to invite her round. Maybe for lunch sometime this week.

Beat.

Has she ever mentioned anything about her situation at home?

DAVID. Is she alright?

BEENA. It's nothing you need to worry about.

AMBER *stands, frozen, scared and enraged, staring at* THE MAN.

AMBER (*to audience*). When I was little,
this man
was the monster under my bed,
the bogeyman in the wardrobe,
the demon in the darkness,
the vampire outside my window.
I'd sleep with the light on,
praying I wouldn't become his prey.

Now,
he is real.

And I watch him.
I watch him as he tends to his rose bush,
wondering if his daughter is buried under it,
and my heart starts beating so fast
I find it hard to catch my breath.

RUBY *enters.*

RUBY. Mum needs you.

AMBER. What time is it?

RUBY. She's been at work all day and you're sitting up here being a lazy cow.

AMBER. I wasn't /

RUBY. I don't want to hear it. /

RUBY *leaves*.

AMBER (*to audience*). That's Ruby.
Bad moods follow her around like a bad smell.
Marriage –
She said I was too young to understand
but I did.
She talked of honour,
respecting our parents,
I screamed in her face
told her to wait
to fight
marry who she wants
when she wants.
I begged her to fight.

AMBER. Love you like apple loves crumble.

RUBY. Love you like sock loves foot.

AMBER. She didn't
and we became strangers
overnight.

SURINDER. Amber…

Amber, can you check the receipt? /

AMBER (*looking at* RUBY). Couldn't you have done it? /

RUBY. Stop your backchat and just do it. /

AMBER. What's up with you? /

RUBY. You. /

AMBER. What have I done? /

RUBY. You do my head in. /

SURINDER. Amber. The receipt.

AMBER. Two lots of four-pint milk, three pounds and thirty pence. One bag of sugar, one pound twenty-five. Ribena, one pound thirty-five, twelve-pack of crisps, one pound thirty-seven. /

SURINDER. They were both reduced to half-price?

AMBER. Yep, half-price... PG Tips, three pounds ninety-five. Twelve eggs, two pounds fifty-five, two loaves of bread reduced, sixty pence each... So that came to fourteen pounds and eighty-five pence. You gave fifteen pounds and you got fifteen pence change.

SURINDER. Yes that's right. Ruby, will you check. /

AMBER. Why does she have to check it? /

SURINDER. Just to make sure. /

Annoyed, AMBER *gives* RUBY *the receipt.* RUBY *barely looks at it.*

RUBY. It's just as she said, Mum.

SURINDER. Okay. Good.

AMBER (*to audience*). And now, she can relax.

HARBANS *enters.* RUBY, AMBER *and* SURINDER *serve and make dinner. It's a swift, quiet, clean operation.*

(*To audience.*) Dad's back.
Turn the volume down,
turn the telly off.
Don't say a word.
Can't he wait?
Five minutes,
just five minutes.
Standing in the doorway,
swaying and
spitting demands.
Mum – exhausted –

rolls out chapattis.
I stir the curry.
Ruby serves.
We serve.
Here to serve.
Dad eats.
I want to scream the house down.

They eat.

Can you sign this? There's a school trip next term.

HARBANS. Where?

AMBER. Peak District.

HARBANS. To do what?

AMBER. Look at rocks.

HARBANS. Can't afford it.

AMBER. It's free, just need to put an 'X' here.

(*To audience*.) I always add his name later.

HARBANS *reluctantly signs the letter.*

I should teach you to write your name.

HARBANS. Don't need you to teach me anything.

RUBY. Can't keep signing your name with an X.

HARBANS. I can do what I like.

AMBER. I'll teach Mum.

HARBANS. She doesn't need to learn anything either…

Put some tea on – (*Mumbles*.) you're doing my head in.

RUBY *and* AMBER *don't move*.

RUBY. Go on then.

AMBER. He's talking to you.

RUBY. He's talking to you.

HARBANS. Amber, are you deaf? Hurry up. Not too much
    arrowroot – it was bitter last time. (*To* SURINDER.) How
    much did you make today?

SURINDER. I don't know. The girls will work it out.

HARBANS. Did you get paid today?

SURINDER. No.

HARBANS. Why?

SURINDER. Some problem at the bank.

HARBANS. When will they pay you?

SURINDER. I don't know.

HARBANS. Well, find out. Otherwise, I'll go down there and
    ask myself. (*Beat*.) Amber, have you looked at the post?

AMBER. No not yet.

HARBANS. Why not?

RUBY. I'll do it.

    She gives AMBER *a look.*

AMBER. What?

RUBY. Whatever.

    RUBY *reads the letter.*

HARBANS. Who is it from?

RUBY. The council.

HARBANS. What does it say?

RUBY. Give me a minute… They're cutting your benefits.

SURINDER. Can they do that?

RUBY. They can do whatever they like.

SURINDER. We barely have enough as it is.

HARBANS. There must be a mistake. Amber, you take a look.

RUBY. Jesus Christ.

RUBY *shoves the letter in* AMBER*'s hand.* AMBER *quickly scans the letter.*

AMBER. That's what it says, Dad.

HARBANS. Call tomorrow. Make an appointment. You tell them it's a mistake.

AMBER. It's not a mistake. They're doing it to everyone.

HARBANS. You want food on the table? You want clothes on your back?

Then you call tomorrow. You hear me.

You hear me, Amber?

AMBER. Yes, okay.

HARBANS. You call the Jobcentre tomorrow.

SURINDER. She said she would.

HARBANS. Was I talking to you?

AMBER (*to audience*). Milky tea starts to simmer.

HARBANS: The tea!

AMBER (*to audience*). Starts to heat up.

SURINDER. The tea!

AMBER (*to audience*). Starts to boil over.

RUBY. The tea!

HARBANS. Stupid girl.

AMBER. Sorry.

HARBANS. Stupid! You're useless.

RUBY. I'll clean it up

HARBANS. I'm going out.

SURINDER. Again? You've only been home five minutes. When will you be back?

HARBANS. When I feel like it.

HARBANS *exits*.

SURINDER. Where is he?

AMBER. Nearly at the bottom of the street.

SURINDER. Good.

She takes a little brown envelope out of her bag. She opens it and begins to count the money inside. She takes a bundle of notes and stuffs it down her bra.

Can't have him drink it all away.

Silence.

…Can I see it?

AMBER. See what?

SURINDER. My name. Written down. Write my name in English. I just want to see what it looks like.

AMBER *writes her name*.

What are the letters?

The letters are projected onto the stage.

AMBER. S. U. R. I. N. D. E. R. R. A. I.

SURINDER. He's right. It's too late for me to learn new things now.

AMBER. It's not.

RUBY. It's not, Mum.

AMBER. Just watch.

As AMBER *writes the letters are projected onto a wall.* SURINDER *watches*.

Your turn.

SURINDER *hesitates. Looking up at the large writing on the wall*.

SURINDER. I'm tired.

AMBER. Just try.

SURINDER. Some other time.

AMBER. Try.

RUBY. Just try, Mum.

SURINDER. Leave it, I said!

RUBY. Leave it, Amber. It's okay, Mum. (*To* AMBER.) Why do you have to stress her out? Can't you see she's tired. You always do this.

AMBER (*to audience*). Fear turns to anger and that's the end of that.

The writing on the wall disappears.

JAS *enters*.

Ruby is married to Jas.
A quiet man.
A kind man.
A gentle man.

JAS. How's school?

AMBER. Yeah good. They want me on the running team again.

JAS. Go on, our kid.

RUBY. Like running's going to get you anywhere.

AMBER. Shut your face.

RUBY. Stop being so defensive.

AMBER. Stop being such a bitch!

JAS. Okay, guys, calm down.

RUBY. You're the bitch.

AMBER. No, you're the bitch.

JAS. Seriously, you two, chill.

Beat.

So, does this mean you'll be competing in races, like last year?

AMBER. My teacher thinks I've got a shot at being on the British Team. /

JAS. No way, that's amazing, so you'll be at the Olympics?

AMBER. Yeah… I mean eventually, one day, hopefully. I mean you never know…

JAS. The Olympics… Rubes… you listening…? The Olympics!

RUBY (*to* JAS, *with bite*). I heard. I'm right here. (*To* AMBER.) You won't be allowed. He'll never let you. /

AMBER. What's it to you! /

RUBY. I'm just saying. /

JAS. You should be really proud. Wish I was good at something.

AMBER (*pause*). Ruby's right. Dad already said no.

JAS. What?

AMBER. It's fine. I'm over it.

JAS. But running's your, you know, *thing*…

Let me know if I can do anything.

RUBY. Oh charming, where's all this support when your mother's breathing down my neck?

JAS. What do you mean?

RUBY. Forget it.

(*To* AMBER.) You won't be allowed to do it. He'll never let you.

(*To audience*.) I had dreams too you know.
Working-class girl done good
picture in the local paper.
I was… exceptional.
Dad got mad.
Someone, somewhere,
told him that girls do x, y, z at university.
That so-and-so's daughter did x, y, z
and now she's

run away,
got pregnant,
doing drugs.
He was told,
you need to hold on to your daughters,
keep them close
get them married
and there was no one to stop it.

Mid-December
No shoes,
no jacket
I ran.
Out the house
I ran.
Slipping and sliding
I ran.
Cutting and bleeding
I ran.
Stumbling and falling
I ran.

And then...
Dad
Hair
Grabbed
Pulled
Pulling.

Me
Screaming
Sliding
Slipping
Skin
Scrapping

Neighbours
Looked.

Curtains
twitched.

Everyone
stayed
inside.
She *can't* be allowed to run.

(*To* AMBER.) He'll never let you

and don't even think about going behind his back.
He'll find out.
He always does.
and when he does
he'll kill you.

AMBER *in bed. She falls back. A cacophony of sounds and images. All her fears up close and real.* THE MAN, TARA *and* DAVID *together, being buried under a rose bush.*

TARA. It was the best holiday ever.

RUBY. He always does, and when he does, he'll kill you.

DAVID. I'm so glad it was just the two of us.

RUBY. And when he does, he'll kill you.

TARA. I've never felt this way about anyone.

DAVID. Me neither.

RUBY. He'll kill you.

TARA. I've never felt this way about anyone.

SURINDER. It was your fault.

DAVID. Me neither.

SURINDER. You did this.

RUBY. He'll kill you.

DAVID. I love you.

SURINDER. Look at me. Look at what you did.

RUBY. He'll kill you.

AMBER *falls, she sinks, beneath the ground.*

THE MAN *is digging. She is underneath the rosebush. She claws and claws and claws, trying to get out.*

AMBER. *Help me! Ruby!*

RUBY *appears. She stands, staring, not moving.*

Ruby! Ruby!

THE MAN *reaches through the earth, she screams.*

(*To audience.*) School.

A revolving day of lessons.

(*To audience.*) Before I started secondary school Ruby gave me the low-down on every teacher… The nice ones…

TEACHER 1. No homework for the rest of the term!

AMBER (*to herself*). YES!!!!

Beat.

The strict ones…

TEACHER 2. No talking. No chewing. No smirking. No daydreaming.

AMBER. The inspiring ones…

TEACHER 3. Remember what Gandhi said?

AMBER (*uninspired*). Be the change you want to see…

TEACHER 3. Exactly!

AMBER. The boring ones…

TEACHER 4 (*deadpan*). Rock formations.

Turn to page one of your textbooks.

AMBER. I don't know why he bothers.

TEACHER 4 (*deadpan*). Rocks. There are three kinds of rock…

AMBER. And then there's Mr Jones, who's in a league of his own.

MR JONES. Who can tell me what a revolution is…?
Anyone…? No…? No one…?

AMBER. He bounds round the classroom like an excited puppy.
Ruby insisted he'd make me love history. He won't.

(*To* TARA *and* DAVID.) What is the point of this? Learning
about King Blah-blah back in the whatever century bores me
to death.

DAVID. Mr Jones is fun though.

TARA. I thought his one-man re-enactments of Henry VIII and
all his wives was fab.

MR JONES *doing his one-man re-enactment.*

MR JONES. Divorced, beheaded, died, divorced, beheaded,
survived!

AMBER. None of it's relevant. What's the point of learning
about the past, none of it relates to the present.

TARA. Try opening your third eye, Amber. You can always
learn from the past.

DAVID. Here she goes.

MR JONES.…Okay. A revolution is…The forcible overthrow
of a government or social order in favour of a new regime. It
can be split into eight stages.

As he reads the words are projected around the stage.

Restlessness, dissatisfaction, control, momentum,
honeymoon, terror, overthrow, peace.

I like to call this 'the anatomy of a revolution', your
homework is to elaborate on each stage.

*Collective groan from the class. The words take up the entire
space.*

AMBER (*to audience*). One word leaps out.
Overthrow. Overthrow. Overthrow.
Something stirs inside,
makes me feel like I have
superpowers…

I feel restless,
my feet need to fly…

Revolution…
Forcible overthrow…
A new regime.

A buzzing, pulsing of lights.

SURINDER. It wasn't your fault.

AMBER. I shouldn't have asked you to talk to him. If you hadn't have tried to convince him he wouldn't have hurt you. /

SURINDER. None of this is your fault.

MR JONES *stands in front of her.*

MR JONES. Your time is coming. Stay strong.

AMBER. What, sir?

MR JONES. It's lunch time. Everyone else has left. Go.

AMBER. Oh yeah. Sorry, sir.

(*To audience.*) David lives on a tree-lined street.

The streets are wider.
The houses bigger.
Breathing feels easier here.

DAVID. Mum?

BEENA. Oh hi, love.

DAVID. I invited Amber and Tara. Is that alright?

BEENA. Yeah of course. I'll fix you all some lunch. Nothing fancy. I hope sandwiches and crisps are okay?

TARA. Yeah great.

AMBER. Perfect. Thank you.

BEENA. Do you want to help me, Amber?

AMBER. Er… sure.

BEENA *and* AMBER *alone.*

(*To audience*.) She's that girl.
Fell-in-love-at-fifteen girl.
Pregnant-at-sixteen girl.
She's that girl.
The-one-who-everyone-talks-about girl.
The-one-who-can't-shake-off-her-past girl.
The-one-everyone-fears girl.
Because-she's-not-ashamed girl.
The proud girl.
Despite-her-past girl.
The-one-they-wish-would-disappear girl.
The fighter girl.
The-one-who-can-corrupt girl.
Holds-her-head-up girl.
Sticks-her-middle-finger-up girl.
Laughs-too-loudly girl.
Doesn't-know-her-place girl.
Should-know-her-place girl.
Takes-up-space girl.
Proudly-stands-tall girl.
Not-moving-for-no-one girl.
Not-apologising-for-nothing girl.
Owning-her-right-to-be-here girl.
Not-cowering-girl.
Lifting-up-others girl.
Giving-the-voiceless-a-voice girl.
Despite-everything-she-survived girl.
And boy does that scare some folk.

BEENA. How's your mum?

AMBER. Okay.

BEENA. We've got loads of new classes starting at the community centre. It would be lovely to see her.

AMBER. I'll tell her.

BEENA. It would be great for her to come down, meet new people, make some friends.

AMBER. I'll let her know.

BEENA. Good... and how you doing?

AMBER. Alright.

BEENA. David told me about the athletics team. I'm sorry.

AMBER. I'm over it.

BEENA. Are you?

AMBER. Yeah.

BEENA. I'm not convinced.

AMBER. Well I am.

BEENA. You don't see any ways around it?

AMBER. Nope.

BEENA. I remember your teacher last year, what's her name...

AMBER. Miss Sutton?

BEENA. Yeah, she was saying you were going to be the next big thing...

AMBER. It is what it is.

BEENA. Your mum and dad not like you doing it?

AMBER. Mum doesn't mind... it's just my dad.

BEENA. You can't convince him?

AMBER. You don't know what it's like.

BEENA. So what's it like?

Silence.

I remember talking to Ruby, you know, before she got married.

She found things hard too. I know you've not had it easy, the two of you.

AMBER *takes a moment*.

AMBER. It's like prison.

Beat.

It's Mum. She's the one that gets it. I can take it. She can't.

BEENA. She gets what?

AMBER. Nothing.

BEENA. I've been there you know. I know what you're going through.

AMBER. Yeah?

BEENA. Yeah. So I get it.

Silence.

I'm going to ask you two questions okay. And you don't have to answer now. Just think about them.

AMBER. Okay.

BEENA. If there was nothing standing in your way... What sort of life do you want to live? And second, what sort of woman do you want to be? And when you've figured that out. Go for it and don't let anyone stop you.

AMBER *walks home.*

AMBER (*to audience*). What sort of life do I want to live?

What kind of woman do I want to be?

Like Beena.

In charge, like Beena.

Strong like Beena.

Overthrow. Overthrow. Overthrow.

Home.

AMBER *notices* HARBANS. *Tries to creep past him.*
HARBANS *is sitting on a chair. Drunk.*

HARBANS. I see you.

She pauses. Still hiding.

Suit yourself.

She continues on upstairs quietly.

AMBER *is reading, immersed in the pages of a history book.*

HARBANS *is dozing on a chair, he has nightmares. He groans calling out. Their words overlap.* AMBER *trying to drown out* HARBANS.

AMBER. People feel restless… /

HARBANS. Stop… /

AMBER. Dissatisfaction spreads… /

HARBANS. Stop it… /

AMBER. They prepare to fight. /

HARBANS. No… No… no… /

AMBER. Accepting all they will lose. /

HARBANS. Help… Mum… Mum… /

She can't concentrate. HARBANS' *nightmare disturbs her.*

Mum! Mum… Mum?

He wakes. Terrified. He picks up a bottle and drinks. Silence.

AMBER (*to audience*). A new day. Jobcentre. With Dad.

JOB CENTRE WORKER. It's not a cut. It's all your benefits in one lump sum.

AMBER. But I don't get it because there will be less money than we get now.

JOB CENTRE WORKER. It's pretty much the same.

AMBER. It's not the same. It's less. We barely make ends meet as it is.

JOB CENTRE WORKER. You just have to manage your money better. Can you manage that?

AMBER. Erm… yeah.

JOB CENTRE WORKER. I can refer you to the money-advice service, to help with money management. Does your dad want to sign up?

AMBER. Are the classes in English?

JOB CENTRE WORKER. At the moment, yes.

AMBER. Then no.

JOB CENTRE WORKER. So I can put down he's declined the referral?

AMBER. Well… he can't speak English so he won't understand anything…

JOB CENTRE WORKER *rolls their eyes while typing on the computer.*

JOB CENTRE WORKER. Is that alcohol I can smell on his breath?

HARBANS *and* AMBER *alone outside the Jobcentre.*

HARBANS. You're useless. You didn't translate properly. What's the point of school if you can't do these basic things.

AMBER. If they're so basic, why can't you do them yourself?

HARBANS. You speak to me like that again, and I'll break every bone in your body.

AMBER *reels in shock.*

AMBER (*to audience*). School.

AMBER *bumps into* GEMMA. *She stands in her way.*

GEMMA. What?

AMBER (*mimics*). What?

GEMMA. Can I pass?

AMBER (*mimics*). Can I pass?

AMBER *attempts to intimidate her a little longer and then lets her pass.*

(*To audience.*) Don't be fooled.
Don't look at me like that.
Gemma Griffin
thinks she's all that.
Rich mum and dad,
little Miss Perfect.

Acts all shy,
victim-like –
couldn't be
further from the truth.
She gives as good as she gets,
and that's a fact.

She thinks she's all that.

I know what she's thinking,
looking down on me.
I see her,
she doesn't need to say it,
I can just tell.
'I wouldn't say a bad word about anyone' eyes
'I'm so innocent' face
'I'm minding my own business' *hair*
I see it.
It's a fact.

She thinks she's all that.

Looks at me
like I'm…
like I'm…
Nothing.

Yeah, she thinks she's all *that*.

Home. AMBER *lights the sage candle.*

Breathe in two three four and out two three four breathe in
two three four and out two three four breathe in two three
four and out two three… forget it!

She blows out the candle and flicks through her text books.

(*Reading from a book.*) 'The Art of Revolution. Fighting for
freedom. To do what the heart desires.'

Words leap from the page. Surrounding her.

(*To audience.*) It's all here. The secrets, the plots, the war, the
change, the peace.

HARBANS *enters*.

HARBANS. Amber! /

AMBER (*to audience*). Reading about incredible men and
women risking their own lives for a better life.

HARBANS. Amber! /

AMBER. Tonight it doesn't ignite my fire.
Tonight it doesn't relate.

HARBANS. Amber! /

AMBER. Tonight I feel stupid.
Tonight I feel useless.

HARBANS. Amber! /

AMBER (*to audience*). Tonight I feel foolish for thinking I
could ever escape.

HARBANS. Amber! Come downstairs, I'm hungry. Amber!

BEENA. What kind of woman do you want to become?

AMBER. I don't know!

She throws the books.

A new day. AMBER *is training.*

(*To audience.*) Training before school.
Fourteen stairs
between the ground and first floor of our home.
Sprint up and down the stairs,
Lunge up the stairs two at a time,
jump down,
jump squats.
Be inventive.
The possibilities are endless.
Repeat ten, twenty, thirty times.

THE MAN *comes out of his house. He stands in his garden,
looking at his roses.* AMBER *steps back, frightened. Turns
and sprints up and down the stairs focused, like she's trying
to run away from the fear. Visibly shaken.*

(*To audience.*) School.

MISS SUTTON. I have the letter I promised you. Get it signed for me. Don't let me down!

AMBER. Yes, miss, because it's *that* easy.

MISS SUTTON. Excuse me?
What's going on, Amber?

Silence.

If you don't tell me, I can't help.

AMBER (*to audience*). Why can't I tell her?
Tell her.
Tell her.
Tell her.
Tell her.
Tell her.
I can't.

(*To* MISS SUTTON.) Nothing, miss.

MISS SUTTON. Amber, these are for you. I found them in lost property. I think they should fit.

She hands her a pair of trainers.

Just until you get new ones. Or you could keep them – they look hardly worn.

AMBER. What if someone comes looking for them?

MISS SUTTON. They won't. They've been in the box for ages.

AMBER. Thanks, miss.

MISS SUTTON. No problem.

AMBER *puts on her new trainers*. DAVID *approaches*.

DAVID. Oi, sister from another mister!

AMBER. Brother from another mother!

DAVID. You look great.

AMBER. You what?

DAVID. I mean, the trainers… they suit you.

AMBER. Oh. Yeah not bad aye.

DAVID. Look at you spending a fortune on Nikes.

AMBER. Nah, Miss Sutton gave them to me,

DAVID. Miss Sutton bought you those?

AMBER. She had them in lost property. Watch me fly in these!

DAVID. They're the latest ones. Trust me. I know my Nikes.

AMBER (*to audience, looking at trainers, back at* MISS SUTTON). She wouldn't… Would she?

Home. AMBER *doesn't realise* HARBANS *is home. She's reading* MISS SUTTON*'s letter.*

MISS SUTTON. Dear Mr and Mrs Rai, your daughter is an extremely talented athlete.

AMBER. Home.

She does a happy dance. HARBANS *scares her.*

HARBANS. Good to see you're back on time.

AMBER. Yeah.

HARBANS. Aren't you going to sit here and talk to me?

AMBER. Why?

MISS SUTTON. We feel she would be a real asset to the running team.

HARBANS. Does there have to be a reason? Just sit and talk to your father.

AMBER. I have a test tomorrow.

HARBANS. Okay.

HARBANS *looks vulnerable.* AMBER *can't help feeling sorry for him.*

AMBER. Half an hour then.

HARBANS. Great. How was school?

AMBER. Fine.

HARBANS. I thought we could make chicken and rice on the
weekend.

AMBER. That would be nice.

HARBANS. We'll make it together. Like old times.

MISS SUTTON. We can see Amber having a bright future in
athletics.

AMBER (*beat*). My teacher wants me to join the running team
again.

HARBANS. I thought I made it clear what I thought about all
your running.

AMBER. I know but, I'm the best in my school.

HARBANS. You're not a young girl any more. It doesn't look
good.

AMBER. It'll just be girls.

HARBANS. No boys?

AMBER. It says it in the letter. It's an all-girls team.

HARBANS. But there were boys last year.

AMBER. It changes with the older teams.

(*To audience*.) I know. But the lies just keep coming.

HARBANS. Let me think about it.

AMBER. Really?

HARBANS. Yes, really.

AMBER *looks at the audience. She can't believe it.*

AMBER (*to audience*). Did I hear that right?

The exchange is repeated.

HARBANS. Let me think about it.

AMBER. Really?

HARBANS. Yes, really.

AMBER (*to audience*). One more time. Just to be sure.

HARBANS. Let me think about it.

AMBER. Really?

HARBANS. Yes, really.

AMBER. Amazing.

　　(*To audience*.) This is amazing.

　　DAVID *and* BEENA*'s home*.

DAVID. Can I ask you something?

BEENA. That depends. You want money it's a no, I'm not feeding your McDonald's habit. (*Beat*.) Spit it out, David.

DAVID. What was it like for you, when you had to sneak around with Dad?

BEENA. What's brought this on?

DAVID. I'm just wondering, that's all. I dunno, you and Dad never really speak about it.

BEENA. I think your dad's still a bit scarred from it all to be honest.

DAVID. What do you mean?

BEENA. I invited him round to my house once, after school, no one home. Never seen him so scared. He was like 'if anyone catches us they'll kill us'. I found it thrilling, loved the sneaking around. My big secret.

DAVID. Dad said your dad chased him, Nana and Granddad out your house...

BEENA. Yep. They agreed to come round and help me tell my mum and dad about the pregnancy. I figured as long as they were with me, my dad couldn't hurt me. But he went ballistic. Your nana had to call the police.

DAVID. Did he go to prison?

BEENA. I wish. Never went back after that. Moved in with your dad and your nana and grandad. But we couldn't go anywhere, the entire community was against us. Rich tried, but in the end, it was too much, we were too young. I moved away.

DAVID. Was it worth it? Leaving everyone and everything.

BEENA. Wouldn't change it for the world... wouldn't be the woman I am today.

I see a lot of that fight in Amber. She's holding back now but I feel it. She's a firework that one.

SURINDER *has the letter and is with* AMBER *in her room.*

SURINDER. He really said that?

AMBER. Yes, Mum.

SURINDER. He's changed his mind about the running team? Just like that?

AMBER. Yes. Why do you look so suspicious?

SURINDER. Because I'm always suspicious of your father.

AMBER. Just trust him for once.

SURINDER. Trust him? Have you forgotten what he did when we spoke about all of this before?

AMBER. I think he's changed. I felt it.

SURINDER. Fine. Okay. He's changed. Your father's changed.

She notices AMBER's *books. Picks them up.*

What's this.

AMBER. History homework.

SURINDER. What kind of history?

AMBER. French revolution. How people fought for their freedom.

SURINDER. Sounds interesting.

AMBER. It is.

SURINDER. Tell me more then.

AMBER. Really?

SURINDER. Yes.

AMBER. Okay, well, there are eight stages to a revolution. First people feel restless, this restlessness spreads and the people, the *rebels* start to think about how things can change. Then, and this is the best bit, people come together. Strength in numbers and all that, together they can make a change, but, it's really important that the rebels stick together and keep going, even if they're scared because, eventually they'll be free. Does that make sense?

SURINDER. Of course. It's fantasy.

AMBER. It's not fantasy. It happens. This is fact not fiction.

Silence. SURINDER *bristles.*

AMBER *and* HARBANS *in the kitchen.*

HARBANS. Chicken, in the pot. Add spices. Not too much. You know how to make the thurka?

AMBER. Onion, garlic, ginger, chilli…

HARBANS. Good. Watch it. Make sure it doesn't burn.

AMBER. When can I try some?

HARBANS. Patience. Turn up the volume on the radio. This is my favourite song…

He sings and dances. For her it's almost like being in a fairy tale. SURINDER *watches.*

Have a taste.

AMBER. Oh my god. It's so good!

HARBANS *continues to dance throughout* SURINDER *and* AMBER*'s scene. The music he's listening to becomes fractured and weird as* SURINDER *pours the alcohol away. The dance merges into him looking for his bottles as* SURINDER *pours and then builds into the argument.*

SURINDER. Amber, I need your help.

SURINDER *searches the house and pulls out bottles of alcohol.*

This is your father.

AMBER. Stop, Mum.

She finds another bottle.

SURINDER. This is your father.

AMBER. What are you doing?

SURINDER. This is your father.

AMBER. Put them back.

SURINDER. This is your father.

AMBER. Please, Mum, put them back.

SURINDER. Whisky, Bacardi, rum, beer, gin, vodka. This is your father.

Amber, don't you see. You can't trust him because he can't change. He will never change.

She takes each bottle and tips it down the sink.

AMBER. Mum stop! What are you doing? Stop! /

SURINDER. Let's see, let's see what he does when he can't find his drink.

AMBER. What have you done?

SURINDER. I am restless, Amber. I am *so* restless.

SURINDER *continues to pour alcohol away.* HARBANS *stops dancing and searches for his bottles.*

AMBER *reads from her history book underneath the argument. She stops and starts trying to block out the argument.*

HARBANS. Where are my bottles? /

SURINDER. What bottles? /

AMBER. Control. Rebels gain power but the ruling regime tries to suppress by any means possible. /

HARBANS. You know very well what bottles. /

SURINDER. I don't know what you're talking about. /

AMBER. Politics thrives on manipulation. /

HARBANS. Don't act dumb. /

AMBER. Politics thrives on empty gestures.

SURINDER. Maybe you're too drunk to remember. /

HARBANS. What did you say? /

AMBER. It's all in the politician's character. /

SURINDER. You heard. When was the last time you were actually sober? /

AMBER. Look at what the politician does not what the politician says.

SURINDER. You even turned up drunk to the jobcentre, you're an embarrassment. /

HARBANS. Shut your mouth or I'll shut it for you. /

AMBER *shouts from her room. Her voice is weak.*

AMBER. Leave her alone. Please. /

SURINDER. I hate you! /

AMBER. Stop it. Please, Mum. Stop it. Shhhhhh. /

AMBER *sees* THE MAN *watering his rose bush.*

(*To audience.*) From now on look at what he does not what he says. Always what he does.

BEENA. What kind of woman do you want to become?

AMBER. A strong one!

AMBER *slowly stands. Looking strong. She slowly makes her way towards her parents.*

HARBANS. Those bottles are my medicine. /

SURINDER. Ha! Medicine! /

HARBANS. Don't laugh at me. /

SURINDER. Everyone laughs at you. You're the drunk who sits outside the shopping centre all day every day! /

HARBANS. You shut your mouth. /

SURINDER. I'm not going to take this any more! /

AMBER enters her parents' space. AMBER grows. She's quiet at first and becomes louder. SURINDER watches.

AMBER. Stop it. Stop it. Stop it!!

They stop. AMBER looks at SURINDER.

Rebellions and their rebels. Ordinary people using their voice, speaking out. Risking everything to make a change…

SURINDER looks at AMBER in awe. AMBER steps towards HARBANS.

Stop it, Dad. Leave. Mum. Alone.

HARBANS steps away from SURINDER and towards AMBER.

HARBANS. Don't ever raise your voice to me again. I'll let it go this time. Next time, you won't be so lucky.

Beat.

Forget about joining that running team.

HARBANS leaves. SURINDER and AMBER have a moment. AMBER feels as though she has lost everything. SURINDER looks defiant.

SURINDER. Give me your letter. I'll sign it.

AMBER. Really?

SURINDER. Really. But I want you to do something for me too.

AMBER. Anything.

SURINDER. Teach me to read.

AMBER. I don't really know how to teach someone to read.

SURINDER *looks at* AMBER. *She bristles with frustration.*

Well, I guess we can start with the alphabet.

Beat.

What about Dad?

SURINDER *signs the letter and hands it to* AMBER.

SURINDER. Let me worry about your father.

AMBER (*to audience*). Momentum.
Revolutionaries gain allies.
A revolution is brewing.
It's almost time.

Interval.

ACT TWO

Opening ensemble movement sequence.

MISS SUTTON. Hill training will be hard.

AMBER (*to audience*). Looking ahead.

MISS SUTTON. Focus on running tall.

AMBER (*to audience*). Running tall.

MISS SUTTON. Hill training will make you stronger!

AMBER (*to audience*). Looking ahead.

MISS SUTTON. Head, shoulders, hips and ankles aligned.

AMBER (*to audience*). Pumping arms.

MISS SUTTON. Look ahead short strides lift knees run tall.

AMBER (*to audience*). Lifting knees
Running tall.
Looking ahead
Pumping arms
Lifting knees
Running tall.
Looking ahead running tall.
Pump lift run look.
Look ahead.
Looking ahead.

TILL. I. REACH. THE. TOP.

DAVID. I love hanging round with you.

AMBER. What do you mean?

DAVID. You're not like other girls, we have a laugh.

AMBER (*to audience*). I'm sorry can we rewind that…

DAVID. I love hanging round with you.

AMBER. What do you mean?

DAVID. You're not like other girls, we have a laugh.

AMBER (*to audience*.) Just once more. I promise, it's the last time.

DAVID. I love hanging round with you.

AMBER. What do you mean?

DAVID. You're not like other girls, we have a laugh.

SURINDER. A!

AMBER (*to audience*). My heads been swimming ever since. B!

SURINDER. C.

AMBER. D.

SURINDER. E.

AMBER. F.

SURINDER. G.

AMBER. H for Honeymoon! Revolutionaries gain power!

SURINDER. Next one!

AMBER. Sorry. I.

SURINDER. J.

AMBER. Do you think Dad knows?

SURINDER. No. You worry too much. How would he know?

THE MAN *appears. He remains for the rest of the scene. He stares.* SURINDER *and* AMBER *stare back.*

AMBER. It's just a feeling I get.

SURINDER. There's nothing to worry about. Keep going…

AMBER. K.

SURINDER (*to audience*). When I was little, maybe eight or nine. I remember walking to the market in South Delhi to buy watermelons. The biggest they've got, my mother would say. My sister Rupi and I would run, race each other past the Government High School, looking at the girls with blue and white ribbons in their braids and boys with their slicked-back oiled hair.

How we wished to be one of those girls behind those gates, learning numbers, reading books, writing stories.

AMBER *continues running and* SURINDER *writing*.

W. /

AMBER. I feel like our secret… /

SURINDER. X. /

AMBER. Mine and Mum's… /

SURINDER. Y. /

AMBER. Is bursting out of me…

SURINDER. Z! /

AMBER. I try and act normal. /

HARBANS. What's wrong with you? You're acting strange.

SURINDER. Nothing. All normal.

AMBER (*to audience*). Totally normal.

School.

AMBER *notices* THE MAN *again*.

(*To audience.*) It's just my imagination.

THE MAN *disappears*.

MR JONES. Good work, everyone. Lots of interesting discussions. I think we can whittle it down to three points. What makes a successful revolution? Amber, do you want to start us off?

AMBER. One. It takes time and organisation. Two. Entrenched regimes do not leave quietly. Be prepared to keep fighting and three, strikes are key to gaining psychological power so stand your ground.

MR JONES. And do you have what it takes? Do you have the courage, Amber?

AMBER. What?

MR JONES. Excellent work, Amber. I can see you've been studying hard.

AMBER. Thanks.

MR JONES. Don't forget your homework, everyone. What makes a successful revolutionary?

End of lesson bell. Everyone leaves. AMBER *is left alone.*

Stay strong. All in good time… Enjoy the honeymoon.

AMBER. Sorry, sir?

MR JONES. Really great work this term.

BEENA *enters.*

AMBER (*to audience*). At the community centre with Mum.

BEENA. I'm glad you could come.

SURINDER. He can't find out.

BEENA. He won't. Trust me. Do you have somewhere safe to go?

SURINDER. I think so. We could stay with Ruby. So, what now?

BEENA. I'll talk you through everything.

SURINDER. There's so much to think about.

BEENA. We'll take it one step at a time.

SURINDER. Together the rebels can make a change.

BEENA. What?

SURINDER. Just something Amber said to me.

BEENA *exits*.

AMBER. I'm scared.

SURINDER. Me too.

AMBER. We can't let him win. We have to keep going, Mum.

SURINDER. I know. I know.

AMBER. Repeat after me. We can't lose momentum.

SURINDER. We can't lose momentum.

AMBER. No matter how scared… say it.

SURINDER. No matter how scared.

AMBER. We can do it. I feel it in my bones.

SURINDER. I'm trying. I really am.

AMBER (*to audience*). A strength is building up inside me
    brick by brick
    courage seeps in
    don't ask me how.
    Our momentum has me honeymooning
    left me with a *knowing*.
    Knowing that change must come from me.
    Knowing I do have a choice.
    Knowing that this choice,
    that this change,
    might mean
    my life
    may never
    be the
    same again.

THE MAN, *still on stage, continues gardening*.

SURINDER *continues with the alphabet*.

SURINDER. D.

AMBER. Not 'D'… Look at the straight line. This is O, this is D – see the difference? D has a straight line. O. D. (*She shuffles the papers*.) Which is O and which is D?

SURINDER. This one is 'O' and this one 'D'.

AMBER. Good.

> HARBANS *enters. The mood changes.* AMBER *and* SURINDER *busy themselves with the usual routine.*

(*To audience*.) Dad's back.
Turn the volume down,
turn the telly off.

SURINDER (*to audience*). Don't say a word.
Can't he wait?
Five minutes,
just five minutes.

AMBER (*to audience*). He stands in the doorway,
swaying.

SURINDER (*to audience*). I roll out chapattis.
Amber serves.

I wake up at 5 a.m. every morning.
A flask of tea and a tiffin box with last night's leftovers.
I leave at 6 a.m.
I work twelve hours a day,
dyeing jeans for fancy shops,
with other women like me,
who have husbands like mine.
When I arrived in this country,
there were classes I could have taken.
I could have learned to drive,
I could have learned to read and write.
But he can't read and write,
he doesn't want a thinking wife,
a progressive wife,
a better life
for me,
for us.

AMBER (*to audience*). Him first, he always eats first.

HARBANS. What's going on with you two?

SURINDER (*to* HARBANS). What do you mean?

AMBER (*to* HARBANS). Nothing.

HARBANS. People tell me things. I always find out.

THE MAN, *still on stage, continues gardening*.

AMBER. We know.

(*To audience*.) This is not living.

SURINDER (*to audience*). This is surviving.
One day this will change.

AMBER *reads in her room with* SURINDER *who continues practising the alphabet. Harmony is interrupted by* HARBANS' *nightmares. Both* AMBER *and* SURINDER *listen for a moment before continuing to read. Revolutionary words* (*rebel, fight, overthrow, revolution, momentum, etc.*) *and alphabet letters surround them.*

AMBER (*to audience*). On the outside

It feels like things are
possible
On the outside life feels more hopeful.
Dad's nightmares
are drowned
by dreams
of the good life.
A life where
Mum and I
live with open skies
without towers
and concrete.
Where Ruby and I
laugh like we used to.
Love like we used to.
Space to breathe

    Space to run.
    Space to fly.
    On the outside life feels like it's shifting
    and something is lifting.

SURINDER (*to audience*). But on the inside. /

AMBER (*to audience*). On the inside. /

SURINDER (*to audience*). The moon is in my throat. /

AMBER (*to audience*). The moon is in my throat.
    I think he knows,
    but we
    keep going with the lie /

SURINDER (*to audience*). We keep going with the lie
    and I feel sick with worry.
    But Amber seems calm.

AMBER (*to audience*). I feel sick with worry
    but Mum seems calm.
    We make plans.

SURINDER (*to audience*). We hide evidence.

AMBER (*to audience*). We get our story straight.

SURINDER (*to audience*). But nothing works.

AMBER (*to audience*). The phantom grip that hugs my throat
    just gets tighter…

SURINDER (*to audience*). And tighter.

AMBER (*to audience*). I see her.
    I'm watching.

TARA (*to* DAVID). You're so funny.

AMBER (*to audience*). I'm always watching.
    The way she twirls her hair
    the way she touches his arm.

TARA. Seriously, have you been going to the gym?

DAVID. No.

AMBER (*to audience*). The way she looks at him.
　　The way he looks at her.
　　Makes my blood boil.

TARA. You have!

DAVID. I haven't. Honestly.

AMBER (*to audience*). They don't know I'm watching,
　　but I am.

　　Training. School field. AMBER *is trying to outrun her
　　paranoia about* TARA *and* DAVID, *her fear things won't
　　change and of her dad. A cacophony of scenes. She's not
　　training well. Stumbling, falling, but getting back up and
　　trying again.*

TARA. We hung out all summer.

SURINDER. I don't want to do this any more.

DAVID. I love you, Tara.

HARBANS. I've made the call.

　　THE MAN *appears. Slowly walking towards her.* AMBER
　　stumbles.

AMBER. Go away!
　　Pumping arms
　　Lifting knees
　　Running tall.

TARA. We hung out all summer.

SURINDER. I don't want to do this any more.

DAVID. I love you, Tara.

HARBANS. I've made the call.

　　AMBER *falls.*

AMBER. Stop it! I don't want this repeated.
　　Inhale. Exhale. Inhale. Exhale.
　　Okay, I'm good. It's all good.

TARA. We hung out all summer.

SURINDER. I don't want to do this any more.

DAVID. I love you, Tara.

HARBANS. I've made the call.

AMBER. I didn't ask for this to be played back! Please stop. Stop.

AMBER *stumbles*.

Focus.
Focus on running.
Push it away.
Outrun it.
Push it away.
Outrun it.
Outrun *terror*.

She falls.

AMBER *stands up. She pulls herself together and starts to run*.

Home. SURINDER *is practising writing her name*.

SURINDER. Suh uh ruh…

AMBER. Ruh… That's it.

SURINDER. Shh, let me do it by myself.

AMBER. Sorry. (*Beat*.) I don't know if I can keep doing this.

SURINDER. Why?

AMBER. Why do you think.

SURINDER. It's okay. We're going to be okay.

AMBER. I'm not sure any more. I feel it, everywhere I go, in school, training, it's there. This threat. This knowing that he could…

SURINDER. You don't have to worry.

AMBER. I feel sick all the time.

SURINDER. If he knew, do you really think he'd be keeping quiet? Trust me.

SURINDER *alone. Practising writing her name. Slowly at first, copying* AMBER*'s handwritten example. Letters are projected onto the wall. She writes her name again and again, growing in confidence. Finally doing it by herself, correctly. She smiles, proud of herself.*

HARBANS *enters. The writing begins to disappear. He looks up as the last letter vanishes.*

AMBER (*to audience*). Dad's back.

SURINDER (*to audience*). Turn the volume down.

AMBER (*to audience*). Turn the telly off.

SURINDER (*to audience*). Don't say a word.

AMBER (*to audience*). Can't he wait?
Five minutes?

SURINDER (*to audience*). Just five minutes.

AMBER (*to audience*). Standing in the doorway, swaying.

SURINDER (*to audience*). Exhausted, I roll out chapattis.

AMBER (*to* SURINDER). Do you want me to make them?

HARBANS. No. Yours won't be any good. Leave it to her.

SURINDER (*to* AMBER). Leave it to me.

Serve your father.

AMBER (*to audience*). Dad eats.

SURINDER *and* HARBANS *talk to one another.*

HARBANS. These chapattis are dry.

AMBER (*to audience*). Hot food on her arm.

SURINDER. It's yesterday's dough.

AMBER (*to audience*). Mess on the carpet.

HARBANS. You trying to make me ill?

AMBER (*to audience*). Blood on Mum's head.

SURINDER. It's not bad. Just not fresh. It's from yesterday.

AMBER (*to audience*). Mum running.

HARBANS. You trying to kill me?

AMBER (*to audience*). Kitchen to hallway to lounge.

SURINDER. Let me butter them.

AMBER (*to audience*). Dad, cutting her off.

HARBANS. You think I'm going to eat these?

AMBER (*to audience*). Mum turning.

SURINDER. I'll make new dough.

AMBER (*to audience*). Lounge, hallway, kitchen, stairs.

HARBANS. The rest of my food will get cold.

AMBER (*to audience*). Dad is faster.

SURINDER. I'll put it back in the pot. What more do you want me to do? Nothing is ever good enough.

AMBER (*to audience*). Mum and dads room. Mum gets a suitcase.

HARBANS. What did you just say?

AMBER (to audience). He pushes her against the wardrobe.

HARBANS. You want to leave? You're trying to leave me?

AMBER (*to audience*). Hospital.

RUBY. What have you done?

AMBER. Me?

RUBY. Yes, *you*. None of this would have happened if you weren't so selfish.

AMBER. How was this my fault?

RUBY. All you care about running and doing what you want to do, you don't care about what it means for her.

AMBER, RUBY and JAS watch over SURINDER at the hospital.

AMBER (*to audience*). Ruby is right.
I am to blame.

One word haunts me.
Terror. Terror. Terror.

RUBY. She'll never leave him.

JAS. It's not right, Rubes.
We should spend more time there, look out for Amber.

RUBY. I hate that house. I hate being there.

JAS. We have to do something.

RUBY. I know! Don't you think I know! We can't all come from perfect families like yours.

JAS. My family's not perfect.

RUBY. I didn't ask you to come.

JAS. I wanted to be here for you.

RUBY. Aren't you late for dinner at your mum's? I'm surprised she hasn't sent out a search party.

Home.

AMBER (*to audience*). I make her comfy on the sofa,
try and form a protective shield around her
make her better
make her happy
place a light bulb in every dark thought.
charge her up
give her courage
to leave, something, anything.

School.

I am a hurricane.

TARA, DAVID, AMBER *and* GEMMA *at school.*
HARBANS *and* BEENA *in town.*

HARBANS. Oi. You! /

BEENA. Excuse me? /

AMBER. Oi! Gemma! /

TARA. Just leave it, Amber. /

DAVID. Just let it go, Amber.

HARBANS. You stay away from my wife and daughter, do you hear me? /

AMBER. I warned you, Gemma. /

BEENA. You're Amber's dad? /

AMBER. You're a fat, ugly cow you know that? /

HARBANS. You know who I am, don't act dumb. I'm warning you. /

AMBER. No amount of make-up can fix this whole situation. /

BEENA. Warning me? /

AMBER. What's the matter, Gemma? Cat got your tongue. /

DAVID. Come on, Ambs, leave her alone.

HARBANS. Yes. Stay out of my family's business.

BEENA. I'm not scared of you. /

AMBER. You really do think you're better than everyone else, don't you. /

HARBANS. You should be scared of me. /

AMBER. You should be scared of me. /

BEENA *walks away, strong but shaken.*

TARA, DAVID *and* AMBER. *A continuation of the scene with* GEMMA.

TARA. That wasn't cool.

AMBER. Easy for you to say. (*To* TARA.) She's always nice to you and she's always swooning over you. (*To* DAVID.) Everything's always easy for you two.

DAVID. That's not true.

TARA. No one has a perfect life.

AMBER. You have no idea.

DAVID. So tell us. /

AMBER. You would never understand. /

TARA. Try us. /

AMBER. This isn't like your stupid crystals, Tara, it's real life. /

DAVID. Take it easy, Ambs. /

AMBER. Get lost, both of you. /

DAVID. What have we done? /

AMBER. What haven't you done. /

TARA. What do you mean? /

AMBER. You're never on my side. /

DAVID. What? /

TARA. Yes we are. /

AMBER. No you're not. /

TARA. What are we supposed to do? /

AMBER. Just be on my side! /

DAVID. If you're being out of order, I'm not just gonna stand there and not say anything.

TARA. What were we supposed to say? /

AMBER. Anything, I need my friends. /

TARA. It's not that easy. /

AMBER. Why cos you secretly want me out the way? /

TARA. What? /

AMBER. Yeah, that's right, I see you, Tara. /

TARA. What you're on about. /

AMBER. You don't fool me. I see what you're both doing. /

TARA. This is what I mean. It's not always easy being your friend. /

AMBER. Well excuse me for having emotions. /

TARA. It's true.

DAVID. It is.

AMBER. Nice. I see you've been having some lovely conversations behind my back. /

DAVID. It's not like that. /

TARA. Maybe our energies are too charged for this conversation. /

AMBER. Ha! *Energy*... Just... leave me alone. Both of you.

(To audience.) Revolutions fail when groups split.
I was stupid to believe things could ever change.

A training session.

(To audience.) Runner's high.
It's
euphoria.
A cloud-nine
dreamland
that can last
for days.
Nonstop.
Those days are
rare these days.
Lately I've started to sink
as *it* floats away.
Drowning as I
freestyle panic-crawl

lanes blurring
cheering fading
My happy place
flipped to a nightmare place.

AMBER *struggles. She falls. Gets up, stumbles again.*

AMBER (*to audience*). Christmas supermarket shop.
Don't know why we bother.

SURINDER. Choose whatever you want.

AMBER. I don't mind what we have.

SURINDER. Choose. Have anything you like.

(*To audience*.) This Christmas will be different.
It has to be.

SURINDER *winces in pain. Holding her ribs.*

RUBY. I told you to rest at home. Amber and I could have done
this.

SURINDER. It's good to get out.

RUBY. Have you taken something for the pain?

SURINDER. Yes. Would you stop fussing. Now choose. Food,
drinks… we'll make this the best Christmas ever. (*She picks
up a bottle of pop*.) Didn't you used to like this when you
were little?

RUBY. Pink lemonade. (*To* AMBER.) Remember how we used
to pretend. /

AMBER. It was champagne. /

RUBY. Or sparkling rosé…

A momentary alliance before it gets awkward again.

SURINDER. Good. We're making progress. Put it in the basket.

She winces in pain again.

AMBER (*to audience*). If I hadn't wanted to join the team
If I hadn't asked Mum to stick up for me

If I hadn't spoken to Beena
If I hadn't agreed to a pact
If I hadn't encouraged her
If I hadn't read about revolutions
If I hadn't have wanted to run
If I'd just been content with how life is supposed to be for me
If I'd have just been less... me.

(*To audience*.) Christmas Day.

(*To* SURINDER.) Chocolate eclairs. /

SURINDER. You'll break the fridge if you keep opening and
closing the door every five minutes. /

AMBER. They must be defrosted by now. /

SURINDER. Not yet but they will in a few hours. /

HARBANS. I'm going to the pub.

RUBY. But dinner will be ready soon.

HARBANS *leaves*.

(*Almost shouting after him*.) We're eating at four. Don't be
late.

AMBER (*to audience*). We joke,
Try and have a good time.
I take the eclairs out of the fridge.
Ruby takes the turkey out the oven
We set it all out on the table
with rocks in our stomach.

Four o'clock
we wait.
Four thirty.
Six p.m.
Still waiting.
seven, eight, nine, ten, eleven, twelve
Still waiting.

SURINDER. Call the hospitals.

AMBER (*to audience*). Same for the past four Christmases.

RUBY. No one of his description in the local hospital tonight.

AMBER (*to audience*). Pink lemonade down the sink
untouched eclairs in the bin.
Two thirty.
A knock at the door.

SURINDER (*to audience*). He's back.

RUBY (*to audience*). Dad's back.

AMBER (*to audience*). Dad's back.
He's standing in the doorway
Swaying
Neighbours holding him up.
They found him at the top of the road.
Just lying on the pavement getting drenched.
We lie him on the living-room floor.
Couldn't he have not drunk
for one night
just one night.

RUBY. Don't touch him, Mum, let him wake up in the morning
and see what he's done for himself.

SURINDER. He'll ruin the carpet. Help me pick him up.

They all try lifting him but can't.

Looks like he's staying there for the night. I'll get some
blankets for him.

SURINDER *exits*.

RUBY *and* AMBER *stand over* HARBANS.

RUBY *kicks* HARBANS, HARBANS *groans*.

AMBER. What are you doing?

RUBY. He ruins everything. I hate him.

AMBER. Me too.

AMBER *smiles. This is the* RUBY *she remembers*.

I've missed you so much.

RUBY. I thought you hated me.

AMBER. I thought you hated me.

RUBY. What? /

AMBER. What? /

RUBY. Love you like apple loves crumble. /

AMBER. Love you like sock loves foot. /

RUBY. Love you like moon loves stars. /

AMBER. Love you like mice love cheese. /

RUBY. Love you like boat loves water. /

AMBER. Love you like kite loves sky. /

They look at HARBANS. AMBER *takes a moment and then kicks him. He groans.*

That's for the eclairs.

First race. Projected: 'Interschool games'.

(*To audience.*) First day back after Christmas break.
First official race of the year.
I hold a bit back, like ten per cent.
Everyone goes full pelt at the beginning.
MY trick: save the energy for later.
Give the others some false hope,
then BAM – last twenty metres I charge up.
Trainers sparking as I gain
still in lane
and whizzing past
so fast
they don't even see me
cross the finish line
like a firework.

MISS SUTTON. Amber, you've done it!!! Next up regionals –
one step closer to counties. A chance at being the best under-
seventeen two-hundred-metre runner in the country. You
know who else held that title at your age?

AMBER. Allie Reid.

(*To audience*.) Seriously, she's obsessed.

MISS SUTTON. Exactly! This is your year. I can feel it…
What's wrong? I thought you'd be over the moon.

AMBER. I am, miss. I am.

(*To audience*.) It's just hard to celebrate

when Fear follows me…

BEENA. How are you doing?

SURINDER. Good. I'm managing to put some money away. I
think I'm ready.

THE MAN *stands watching*. AMBER *tries to ignore him*.

BEENA. I'm really proud of you.

SURINDER. What if he…

BEENA. You call me. I'm here for you.

I've done this hundreds of times.

SURINDER. He might come after you.

BEENA. I can handle him.

AMBER (to audience). Fear follows me into school,

every training session…

I have nightmares.
He haunts my dreams and
my every waking moment.

Fear follows me into regionals
Follows me as I win.

Fear follows me
…everywhere.

THE MAN *stares at her, she can't help but stare back*.

AMBER *has* GEMMA *cornered*.

Why won't you fight back?

(*To audience*.) She looks at me.
Trying not to cry.
So I punch her, really hard in the stomach.
I've never hit anyone in my life.
It's soft,
she's soft.

AMBER *is shocked that she's done it*.

GEMMA. Why are you doing this?

GEMMA *pushes* AMBER *to the floor. Her hand in a fist*.

AMBER. Do it. Do it. Hit me.

GEMMA. No, I'm not like you.

GEMMA *walks away. Leaving* AMBER *alone, defeated*.

Home.

AMBER (*to audience*). Dad's back.

SURINDER (*to audience*). Turn the volume down.

AMBER (*to audience*). Turn the telly off.

SURINDER (*to audience*). He stands in the doorway, swaying.

AMBER (*to audience*). No more. The last time. No more
excuses.

SURINDER (*to audience*). He can wait five minutes.

HARBANS. So, all this time you've been lying.

SURINDER. What are you talking about?

HARBANS. You two think you're so clever.

SURINDER. What?

HARBANS. I told you people talk. I've been told you were at
a competition. A sports event. Running. All this time, saying
you were studying. You really think you can get away with
lying.

SURINDER. Talk to her when you've calmed down.

HARBANS. I always said you had the devil inside you.

AMBER (*to audience*). He says no one can help us now.
He says we should have listened.
He goes to punch Mum.

AMBER catches his fist.

SURINDER. Leave it. Leave it! I don't want you to get hurt.

A stand-off between AMBER *and* HARBANS. HARBANS
appears to be shrinking. AMBER *looks stronger than ever.*
She pushes him down.

AMBER (*to* HARBANS). This ends now.

HARBANS *is frozen. He looks small and defeated.*

SURINDER. Call Ruby. Quickly. We're leaving. Now, Amber!
Hurry!

SURINDER *and* AMBER *have their bags packed. They turn
to leave but* HARBANS *is in their way.*

He stands in front of the door. Blocking their way.

HARBANS. Stop. Just listen to me. I'm still your father. Don't
leave, please.

AMBER. I'll call the police if you don't let us leave.

HARBANS. You're not going anywhere.

SURINDER. Get out of the way. (*Louder.*) Get out of the way.
(*She screams in his face.*) GET OUT OF THE WAY!

Everyone is shocked. HARBANS *is speechless.* SURINDER
takes a moment. She grabs AMBER *and they leave.* THE
MAN *is outside on the street.* AMBER *stares at* THE MAN.

(*To audience.*) Is there
a way to break free
without breaking us apart?
Is there
a way you can learn from the past

and heal from the hurt?
Is there
a way to stay together
and still move on?
Is there
a way to forgive the person
who has caused you so much pain?
Maybe
if I'm there to defend.
Maybe
now I'm stronger.
Maybe
he'll change and shift into someone else.
Maybe
he'll become the person he was meant to be.
Maybe
we all can.

AMBER *looks at* SURINDER.

RUBY *and* JAS*'s house*.

RUBY. I should have been there for you.

SURINDER. I should have been there for you.

RUBY. Why did it take you so long to leave? I wanted a choice, Mum. You took that from me.

SURINDER. But Jas is a nice man.

RUBY. Nice isn't enough. I wanted more.

SURINDER. I didn't know how to leave before…

   JAS *enters interrupting their conversation*.

JAS (*to* AMBER). You all right, our kid?

AMBER. I don't know. I feel…

RUBY. What's wrong?

AMBER. I don't know.

JAS. You're gonna be okay. You're safe now. You okay, Amber?

   AMBER *finds it difficult to breathe*.

RUBY. Slowly breathe in… And out… Look at me… In… and out…

AMBER. What if he comes after us?

RUBY. Who? Dad?

AMBER. The Man.

RUBY. He won't. I won't let him come anywhere near us. Trust me. Look at me… love you like birds love to fly.

You're okay.

AMBER. I'm not okay, He's going to come after us.

JAS. Who?

AMBER. The Man.

JAS. What man?

RUBY. Mr Garcha, who lives across the road. The one who murdered his daughter…

AMBER. Dad… Dad… always said… Always said… that he'd come for us if we ever… if we ever…

JAS. Mr Garcha at number forty-two?

RUBY. Yes.

JAS. He wouldn't hurt a fly.

SURINDER. That man is evil, people aren't always what they seem.

JAS. I've known him my whole life. I went to school with his daughters.

Both alive, both doing very well for themselves.

AMBER. How come we don't see the older one? She ran away and Mr Garcha found her and murdered her.

JAS. What? No, she's just moved away, trust me I'm friends with her. I can't believe what you've been told.

The three women sit in silence. Shocked.

SURINDER. All this time.

Beat.

AMBER (*to audience*). Something is changing.

SURINDER (*to audience*). Something is shifting.

RUBY (*to audience*). A weight has been lifted.

MR GARCHA *waves at them. They wave back.*

A wish

SURINDER (*to audience*). I didn't know I had made

AMBER (*to audience*). Has been granted.

He hands them the roses.

MR GARCHA. For your new home.

AMBER *takes the roses.*

AMBER (*to audience*). Ruby lives next to a park.
Running outside
feeling the breeze kiss my skin
life doesn't get much better.

RUBY. I think I need to figure out what I want.

JAS. Okay.

RUBY. I need to figure out who I am.

JAS. Okay.

RUBY. We need to see if we belong together.

JAS. I want to make it work.

RUBY. I know you do.

JAS. I'll always support you. You know that, don't you?

RUBY. Yeah I know.

JAS. So, let me in.

RUBY. I need time.

JAS. Have all the time you need. (*Beat*.) Ruby, do you love me?

RUBY (*beat*). I don't know.

> (*To audience*.) My heart is locked.
> When love has not been in abundance
> you seek it first
> you look for it in every corner of your being.
> Love.
> Love must always come first.

> AMBER, TARA *and* DAVID, *St Martin's Church*.

AMBER. I know I haven't been the easiest person to be around.

TARA. I'm just glad we're talking again.

DAVID. You're lucky we like ya.

AMBER. I'm the lucky one.

TARA. So, I know you're going to laugh but I've got something for you. It's a clear quartz crystal. It's actually known as the master healer because it aligns all your chakras.

> TARA *puts it in* AMBER's *hand*.

AMBER. Thank you. It's perfect.

TARA. It works, trust me.

AMBER. I'm sorry for pushing you away and all the crazy, jealous stuff I was saying.

TARA. We're never gonna judge you.

DAVID. We just want to be here for you.

AMBER. I really don't deserve either of you.

TARA. Come here.

> *Big group hug*.

AMBER (*to audience*). The two of them
    breathing courage
    and love
    into every cell.

Sticking all
the broken pieces
of me
together again.

We talk,
like old times
laugh,
like old times
together again,
like old times.

A new home.

SURINDER. It's only one bedroom but we can make it work.

AMBER. It's perfect, Mum.

SURINDER. We'll make it a home.

AMBER. It's perfect.

(*To audience*.) The old house. I don't know why. Just seems right.

The house is a mess, Dad.

HARBANS. See what becomes of me when you're not here.

Pause.

Just stay for a while.

AMBER. I can't.

HARBANS. Talk to me.

AMBER. I have to go.

HARBANS. Then why did you come?

AMBER. I don't know.

Beat.

What happened to you, Dad?

HARBANS. My life…
not easy.
Orphanage…

Horrible place…
Here…
Promise of a new life.
A better life…
But… no.

I'm… broken.

Broken people… can't love.

It's too late… to learn… to love.

AMBER *stares at him. She keeps her distance.*

AMBER (*to* HARBANS). You're wrong.
It's never
too late
to learn
to love.

(*To audience.*) In these old times
I'm all new
These secrets
They were never meant to be shared.
Dad, lies, violence, threats and Gemma.
Gemma who never deserved any of it.

Gemma Griffin
doesn't think she's all that.
She might have a rich mum and dad
but she doesn't give as good as she gets,
and that's a fact.
Yeah Gemma Griffin
doesn't think she's all that.
We're talking thanks to Tara and David
She's looking at me
I'm looking at her
I see it now.
It's a fact.
Gemma Griffin never thought she was all that
She never looked at me,
like I was…

like I was…
Nothing.
It was all me
those are the facts.

At one point Gemma and I laugh at the same thing
and it feels like the start of something
new.

The new flat. AMBER *is with* RUBY.

Where's Mum?

RUBY *hands her the note. The note is projected onto the walls. 'Amber I gone shop for partee food. I mite b layte. No wory. Mum.'*

RUBY. Look at that.

AMBER. Incredible.

SURINDER *enters with shopping bags.*

We found your note.

SURINDER. Did I write it all correctly?

AMBER. Almost. I'm so proud of you!
Also… are we really having a party?

SURINDER. I bought so many things… /

AMBER *takes the receipt out of the bag starts to read it out loud.*

AMBER. Two meat-feast pizzas, one pound sixty-five each, crisps, multi-pack, one pound fifty…

SURINDER. You don't need to do that any more, I know what I bought… Pizza, crisps, those little sausages you like and the sticks to put them on, dips, oh balloons, and the most special things… you'll like this… chocolate eclairs and pink lemonade.

A housewarming party – starts during above.

AMBER (*to audience*). There has never been music, dancing, laughing, singing, or colours in our home before.

DAVID. I've wanted to give you something for ages.

AMBER. What is it?

DAVID. Open it.

AMBER. A signed photo of Allie Reid! '*To Amber. Good luck in the finals! Much love Allie.*' Oh my God! It's amazing thank you.

DAVID. Turn it over. Read the other side.

AMBER. 'You're more than just my sister from another mister. You know that, right?' It's really special. You know she's my idol.

DAVID. Is that all you liked about it? What about what I wrote?

AMBER. We're like best mates?

DAVID. I didn't want to say anything, but Tara said something about how a life lived with regret is a life half lived or something, and I just knew that, even if nothing can happen, you needed to know.

AMBER. Tara said that?

DAVID. Yeah, sorry, I had to confide in someone.

AMBER. I thought you liked Tara.

DAVID. No... Well I do, just not like that. (*Beat.*) I'd have risked everything to sneak around with you. It's always been you.

They kiss.

AMBER *looks at the audience.*

AMBER (*to audience*). Just once more.

DAVID....It's always been you.

They kiss.

AMBER (*to audience*). I float all the way to the start line.

The race. Projected: 'County Championships'.

SURINDER, TARA, DAVID, RUBY *and* JAS *are all present encouraging her.* AMBER *focuses.*

VOICE-OVER. On your marks. Get ready.

Silence.

Starting gun.

AMBER (*to audience*). Accelerating,
Arms pumping,
Legs driving forward
Into my future
and towards my dreams.

The race slows. AMBER *lands home with* RUBY *and*
SURINDER. *They set up their home; rug, chairs, the roses
from* THE MAN *across the road in a vase.*

The women sit around a table. RUBY *studying.* AMBER
putting on a pair of trainers. SURINDER *reading. The
conversation is quiet, casual, between themselves.*

AMBER *looks at them.* RUBY *and* SURINDER *continue
talking under* AMBER*'s final monologue.*

(*To audience.*) Finally, peace.
We did it.
We rebelled and we won.
My truth.
My story.
No longer bound by secrets
or silenced by fear.
My name is Amber Rai and I am…
no…

She looks back at SURINDER *and* RUBY.

WE are rebels.

Blackout.

The End.

Educational Resources and Activities
Written by Carolyn Bradley
Edited by Oliver O'Shea

These resources are aimed at teachers and educators within English, Drama and PSHE curricula at KS3, KS4 and KS5 levels. They can be used to help students understand the context of the story and themes.

There are suggested activities and prompt questions to help engage students with some of the challenging issues and topics the play raises; these appear in shaded panels, like this one.

We would suggest that you consider whether any of the subjects explored in the play and resources may be triggering for some of your students, and we advise that the resources contain plot spoilers.

Synopsis

Contains spoilers!

Act One

Amber Rai lives in the Palm Wood estate – 'One of the roughest and biggest estates in the country' – with her mum and dad. She has a sister called Ruby who has left home. She talks about the stories she has heard about being unwanted as a baby due to being a girl, and how people prayed and wished she was a boy.

Amber meets with her friends Tara and David on the first day back at school. David looks different after the summer break and Amber is attracted to him. In PE, Amber talks about the running track as being the only space she feels 'free'. Amber's teacher, Miss Sutton, wants Amber to train with the school for the county finals, so that she can go for the English Schools Athletics Championships. Amber says she can't because her dad won't let her.

After school, Tara, David, and Amber go to McDonald's, but Amber is trying to avoid being seen. After Amber runs home, her dad, Harbans, accuses her of lying about where she has been. He is drunk and aggressive. He reminds Amber about 'The Man who killed his daughter – the daughter who shamed the family', a story Amber and Ruby were told as children to scare them into behaving.

That evening, Amber follows the routine of having to read out her mum's shopping receipt to her, as neither of her parents can speak, read or write English. Ruby, Amber and her mum then make and serve dinner for her dad when he returns home. He then goes back out again, and Amber's mum, Surinder, asks Amber to spell out her name in English so she can see what it looks like.

Back in school, Amber's History class starts learning about revolutions, and something stirs within Amber. At David's house for lunch, David's mum, Beena, asks about Amber and her mum, and says she was once in the position Amber's mum is in. She wants Amber's mum to go down to the community centre to meet people. Amber takes her dad to the job centre, and interprets for him in a meeting about their benefits being cut. After he criticises her interpretation, Amber answers back, and her dad threatens to break every bone in her body.

Miss Sutton has given Amber some new trainers which she says are from lost property, to replace Amber's ripped ones. She gives Amber a letter for her parents about allowing her to run. Amber is reading it aloud and her dad hears. He is in a strangely good mood and says he will think about letting her go, which amazes Amber, but when she tells her mum, she is suspicious: 'Amber, don't you see. He can't change. He will never change.'

Surinder pours all of Harbans' alcohol down the sink, and when he returns home he attacks her in a rage. Amber is reminded of the History lessons and the stories of 'rebellions and their rebels' and she interrupts the fight, shouting at her dad to leave her mum alone.

Mirroring Harbans attacking Surinder at home, Amber verbally attacks Gemma, a girl at school, threatening her: 'If you ever say anything about me again. I will end you, you hear me?'

Surinder is looking at Amber's school books in her room and asks Amber to teach her to read English in secret. Amber teaches her slowly, starting their own revolution. Surinder signs the letter, consenting for Amber to take part in running practice after school.

Act Two

Amber continues to train to run, and Surinder continues to learn English. Amber is questioned by her dad again about where she has been after school, and she lies, telling him she has been studying. He emotionally manipulates her by saying, 'I'm just trying to do my best. I'm trying to protect you', and he threatens her by saying that people in the community will tell him things, and he will find out the truth. Amber is scared, but she is still strong, and tells her mum that 'We can't let him win. We have to keep going, Mum.' Surinder goes to the community centre and meets Beena.

Amber trains, but as she runs she is troubled by images of Tara and David, who she thinks are getting closer, and her mum, dad and the Man.

The home routine of Harbans returning home drunk is played out, with Surinder rolling out chapattis and Amber serving her dad. Harbans aggressively criticises Surinder for the chapattis being dry, and she answers him back, saying, 'What more do you want me to do? I'm giving you solutions, nothing is ever good enough.' This enrages Harbans, who then physically attacks her in front of Amber.

Surinder is in hospital, and Ruby blames Amber, saying she is selfish for just focusing on her running. Jas, Ruby's husband, says they should do something to protect Amber and Surinder, and suggests that Surinder can move in with them.

Back home, Amber looks after her mum and tries to make her comfortable. At school, Amber is angry and scared about everything that's happened at home, and takes it out on Gemma, threatening her. In a parallel scene, Harbans bumps into Beena and threatens her, ordering her to stay away from his family. Beena tells him she is not scared of him.

After she has bullied Gemma, Tara and David tell Amber that she was out of order and that it 'wasn't cool'. Amber lashes out, telling them they don't understand what her life is like, and they argue. Tara and David try to understand but Amber pushes them away and they fall out.

At Christmas, Surinder encourages Amber to buy treats and nice food, as she wants this Christmas to be different and for Amber to make some nice memories. Amber doesn't see the point, as her dad drinks more at Christmas and it can be even worse. She reflects on how her running and rebelling against her family has caused her mum harm, and starts to think that Ruby is right, and she should give up being selfish and just look out for her mum more. Amber bumps into Tara and David who try to apologise and make up, but she pushes them away again. She reflects on how revolutions fail when groups split up, and allow terror to rule.

On Christmas Day, Amber's dad goes to the pub, but she asks him to come back by four so they can eat dinner together. He doesn't return, but is brought back hours later by neighbours who found him collapsed at the top of the road. Ruby and Amber kick him angrily as he lies unconscious on the living room floor. Ruby and Amber bond over this moment, and finally talk after years of being estranged. Ruby says she had to distance herself from the family when she moved out, to protect herself, and Amber tells Ruby how much this upset her and how lonely she has been.

At the Interschool Games, Amber races. She wins and is through to the regional finals, but struggles to be happy because of the turmoil in her life. Surinder talks to Beena, and says she is nearly ready to leave Harbans. Amber attacks Gemma again, physically punching her this time.

At home, Surinder is reading with Ruby, and Harbans enters. He is angry, he has found out Amber has been at a running competition. He explodes in a rage at all of them, saying they have the devil inside them. As he goes to hit Surinder, Amber steps in and pushes him down: 'Overthrow, overthrow, overthrow.' They call Ruby, who comes to get them, and they leave with a small suitcase, Harbans begging them to stay.

At Ruby's house, Amber has a panic attack, full of fear that because they've left, the Man will now come after them. Jas tells Amber and Ruby that the Man across the street "wouldn't hurt a fly" and it transpires that the story of the Man murdering his daughter was made up by Harbans, to control them with fear.

Later, Amber is able to train in the park next to Ruby's house. They are embarking on 'a new way of life'. Amber apologises to Tara and David and they make up.

Amber briefly returns home to find her father in a pitiful state. He attempts to tell her about his life, mentioning an orphanage and being beaten. He says he is 'broken' and it's too late for him to learn how to love. Amber tells him it isn't too late, and leaves. Back at Ruby's home, Ruby confronts Surinder about not leaving Harbans sooner, and says she feels angry that she didn't have any choices when she was eighteen.

Amber and Surinder get their own home together and throw a small party. Surinder is more independent, shopping for things herself and knowing what she bought, and she attends classes at the community centre. Amber goes to the national finals to race, and David is there. He confesses his feelings for her, and they kiss. The play ends with three women together, 'Ruby studying. Amber putting on a pair of trainers. Mum reading.' Amber tells the audience they did it, they rebelled and they won: 'We are rebels.'

This synopsis was prepared from the rehearsal draft of the script and may differ from the final version of the playtext.

Principal Characters

Amber is fifteen years old and a passionate and talented runner, but she lives her life in fear of her father. Harbans inflicts terror on his family, through physical and emotional abuse. He controls Amber's behaviour through fear and guilt, to the extent that she can't have normal teenage friendships and participate in extracurricular sports without lying to him. Amber acts as the translator and interpreter for her parents, who can't read or speak English. Amber wants to protect her mum but feels helpless, until she begins to teach her how to read. Amber can be a bully herself, picking on and attacking Gemma, another student at school, which is a way of lashing out due to her own experiences of trauma. Later, Amber realises her actions are unacceptable. Amber is inspired by learning about rebellions in History at school and begins her own revolution.

Key quote:

> No matter how small or quiet
> I'm expected to be at home,
> I find my voice on the running track
> It's where I'm truly alive.

Harbans is Amber's dad, in his late forties. He is an alcoholic and abuses his wife and daughters emotionally and physically. He cannot read or speak English, and his actions perhaps partly stem from his own feelings of inadequacy. He has experienced trauma himself, and briefly refers to his own damaged upbringing where he experienced child abuse and neglect. At times he appears to have changed and is nice and loving towards Amber, but this is part of his manipulative character and his desire to control his family's behaviour. He is obsessive about his family's reputation in the community, often accusing his wife Surinder of wanting to leave him, and Amber of lying to him. He appears to be respected by peers in the Temple and in the community and puts this reputation above the basic needs of his family.

Key quotes:

> You speak to me like that again, and I'll break every bone in your body.

> My life... not easy. Orphanage... Horrible place... Here... Promise of a new life. A better life... But... No.

Surinder is Amber's mum, in her early forties. She is damaged by her own experiences of childhood trauma, where she was told she was unwanted because she was a girl. She is a victim of domestic abuse and coercive control and has not been able to learn to speak, read or write English, thus disempowering her further. She works very long hours in poor conditions and waits on her husband at home. Through Amber, and with Beena's support, she learns to read and write, and slowly becomes stronger. After she is brutally attacked and hospitalised by Harbans, she finally leaves with Amber, and they move in temporarily with Ruby. By the end of the play, Surinder is able to write notes to Amber in English, read simple books, and attends classes at the community centre with Beena where she is making friends.

Key quote:

> When I arrived in this country, there were classes I could have taken. I could have learned to drive, I could have learned to read and write. But he can't read and write, he doesn't want a thinking wife, a progressive wife, a better life for me, for us.

Ruby is Amber's older sister, in her early twenties, and married to Jas. Her marriage was arranged when she was eighteen, and although Ruby now has a good relationship with Jas and he is loving and kind, she still resents the fact that the marriage wasn't her choice. She wanted to go to university but was not allowed. Ruby recounts a story to the audience of when she tried to escape from home but her dad pulled her back by her hair, so she has also experienced emotional and physical abuse. She is estranged from Amber, whom she frequently berates for being 'selfish' and focusing on her running instead of looking out for her mum. At the end of the play, Ruby has been more open with Jas, admitted she needs time to work out if she does love him or not, and is studying, suggesting she has achieved her goal of university.

Key quotes:

> Someone, somewhere, told him that girls do x, y, z at university. That so-and-so's daughter did x, y, z and now she's run away, got pregnant, doing drugs.

> I need to figure out who I am.

David is fifteen years old, Amber's closest friend at school and a boy she is secretly attracted to. He is in the running club, and the daughter of Beena. He is worried about Amber and wants to help her but doesn't know how, and Amber's jealousy about his friendship with Tara causes tension. He doesn't understand why Amber isn't allowed to be seen with him, go to McDonald's or to the running club. He knows that Beena left David's dad and he questions her about this, to try and understand more. David reveals at the end of the play that he also has feelings for Amber and they kiss.

Key quote:

> It's Amber. I'm worried about her. Her dad won't let her join the running team this year…

Tara is fifteen years old and Amber's close friend at school. She is interested in holistic therapies and wants to help Amber through her use of scented candles and crystals, and although she means well, Amber finds this frustrating. She knows that something is up with Amber and wants to help but doesn't know what to do. Tara comes from a more privileged background and perhaps is unable to fully comprehend Amber's situation, but she is a good and loyal friend. It is suggested she too has feelings for David, but ultimately David chooses Amber.

Key quote:

> A sage candle. It'll help cleanse any negative energy by balancing out your chakras. You should light it when you meditate...

Beena is David's mum, in her early forties. Beena met David's dad at the age of fifteen and was pregnant at sixteen. She was pressured into having an abortion, but didn't, and when everyone found out, she was shamed, and David's dad left her. She is a strong woman who now uses her strength to help women such as Surinder. She leads classes at the community centre for women. She is non-judgemental and empathetic. She knows about Amber and Surinder's situation, and tries to help, before they finally accept and Beena helps them escape Harbans.

Key quote:

> If there was nothing standing in your way... What sort of life do you want to live? And second, what sort of woman do you want to be?

Themes and Topics

Revolution and Rebellion

A revolution is… The forcible overthrow of a government
or social order in favour of a new regime. It can be split
into eight stages. Restlessness, dissatisfaction, control,
momentum, honeymoon, terror, overthrow, peace.

AMBER (*to audience*). One word leaps out.

Overthrow. Overthrow. Overthrow.
Something stirs inside,
makes me feel like I have superpowers…
I feel restless,
my feet need to fly…

Amber learns about revolutions in her History lessons with Mr
Jones, and this sparks something inside her. As she reads, she
becomes more and more inspired and intrigued, and this leads
her and Surinder to stage their own revolution against Harbans'
tyranny.

A revolution happens when there is anger and dissatisfaction
with the current leadership or regime, which is trying to control
a group forcibly. This leads to short bursts of rebellion, violence
or protest.

There can be 'flashpoints' in a revolution – such as a war or acts
of violence against the people, which leads to a more urgent
need for action and the revolution gains momentum. This brings
the revolutionary action to a head, speeding up the pace of the
revolution. (alphahistory.com/vcehistory/what-is-a-revolution)

Revolutions can lead to war – as two opposing forces are struggling for power, and sometimes the forces will directly clash, like at the Bastille (France, July 1789) and the Winter Palace (Russia, October 1917). Once they have overthrown power, the revolutionaries must start a new regime, which will include solving the problems of the old regime and developing new rules for society. There have been revolutions and rebellions since time began, but the major revolutions which are considered to the five great revolutions of the modern world are: the English Revolution (1649), American Revolution (1776), French Revolution (1789), Russian Revolution (1917) and Chinese Revolution (1949).

- What revolutions from history have you studied? Why did they happen? What was the outcome?

- Is a rebellion the same as a revolution? Do the words have different connotations?

- Is Amber a rebel or a revolutionary?

- What first inspires Amber about revolutions?

- Does the narrative of *Run, Rebel* follow the eight stages of a revolution: *Restlessness, Dissatisfaction, Control, Momentum, Honeymoon, Terror, Overthrow, Peace*? Can you identify these moments in the story?

Women and Sport

AMBER. My teacher wants me to join the running team again.

HARBANS. I thought I made it clear what I thought about all your running. [...] You're not a young girl any more. It doesn't look good.

Amber is a talented runner, but is not allowed to go to the school running training because of her father's view that women should not participate in sport. He believes this will bring shame on the family, and now she is growing up she needs to behave more 'respectably'.

Miss Sutton, Amber's PE teacher, is a positive female role model, and believes in Amber's ability and that she should have these opportunities. Miss Sutton buys Amber trainers when hers rip, and sends a letter home to her parents to explain how important it is that Amber participates. Miss Sutton also likens Amber's talent to Allie Reid, a former student and professional runner.

The United Nations says sport has the power to change lives, and 'women in sport defy gender stereotypes and social norms, make inspiring role models, and show men and women as equals.' (unwomen.org/en/news/in-focus/women-and-sport)

However, research suggests that teenage girls are more disengaged from sport than teenage boys, with body image, self-belief and perception of capability all being cited as reasons.

(womeninsport.org/research-and-advice/our-publications/ reframing-sport-for-teenage-girls-tackling-teenage-disengagement)

Several other reasons also come up in this research, such as: 'that girls are not as competitive; that sport is not important for girls; that they will never be as good at it compared to boys; that sport can be at odds with femininity. Add to that the harassment and unwanted attention teenage girls are subject to when exercising and quite simply, taking part becomes a burden, instead of bringing freedom and joy.'

Sport England research suggests that faith also influences participation in sport, stating: 'For some faith groups, there's also a larger difference between levels of physical activity between men and women. This is influenced by certain cultural expectations around what they should wear or how they behave.' (sportengland.org/research-and-data/research/faith-groups)

This goes some way to explain Harbans' attitude, which is influenced by his understanding of cultural expectations of what women should do and how they should behave. Campaigns such as This Girl Can are committed to reducing inactivity and getting all women and girls, regardless of background, active and enjoying sport. (sportengland.org/funds-and-campaigns/this-girl-can)

- What could change Harbans' mind about Amber taking part in sport?

- Is Harbans' attitude an example of gender discrimination or his religious belief?

- Is PE at your school inclusive for everyone?

- What could change in schools and nationally to encourage more girls to take part in sports?

- Is it easier for David to be in the running team than Amber? Why?

- Does Miss Sutton really understand why Amber can't take part?

Domestic Abuse

HARBANS. You're useless. You didn't translate properly. What's the point of school if you can't do these basic things?

AMBER. If they're so basic, why can't you do them yourself?

HARBANS. You speak to me like that again, and I'll break every bone in your body.

Ruby, Amber and Surinder are all victims of domestic abuse. There are different kinds of abuse, such as:

- *Physical abuse:* slapping, hitting, punching, scalding, burning, force-feeding or starving.

- *Emotional abuse:* intimidation, coercion, harassment, threatening, bullying, preventing choice or self-expression.

- *Sexual abuse:* rape or attempted rape, non-consensual touching or penetration, any non-consensual sexual activity, indecent exposure, the taking or sending of indecent photographs, sexual teasing or innuendo.

- *Neglect:* denying access to food, shelter, clothing, heating or stimulation; isolating a person; not taking account of educational or social needs; preventing a person from making their own decisions.

- *Financial abuse:* theft, fraud, scamming, preventing a person from accessing their own money, undue pressure to spend money.
(scie.org.uk/safeguarding/adults/introduction/types-and-indicators-of-abuse)

Women's Aid defines domestic abuse as: 'An incident or pattern of incidents of controlling, coercive, threatening, degrading and violent behaviour, including sexual violence, in the majority of cases by a partner or ex-partner, but also by a family member or carer. It is very common. In the vast majority of cases it is experienced by women and is perpetrated by men.' (womensaid.org.uk/information-support/what-is-domestic-abuse)

In the play, Ruby is angry at Surinder for not leaving Harbans sooner. There are many barriers facing women who experience domestic abuse which prevent them from leaving their abuser, such as financial barriers, but mainly fear and danger. 41% (37 of 91) of women killed by a male partner/former partner in England, Wales and Northern Ireland in 2018 had separated or taken steps to separate from them. (womensaid.org.uk/information-support/what-is-domestic-abuse/women-leave)

Abuse can be a learned behaviour, something which some perpetrators may have experienced in their own lives growing up. Domestic abuse stems from a desire to gain power and control over other people. It is important to understand that the decision to abuse someone is a choice, and people could also choose not to. (thehotline.org/identify-abuse/why-do-people-abuse)

- Looking at the examples above, what types of abuse do Amber, Surinder and Ruby experience?
- Why would it have been difficult for Surinder to leave Harbans?
- Should Amber's school have noticed signs that she was being abused?
- Should the police or social services have been involved in Amber's home life?

Friendship and Relationships

DAVID. I didn't want to say anything, but Tara said something about how a life lived with regret is a life half lived or something, and I just knew that, even if nothing can happen, you needed to know.

AMBER. Tara said that?

There are complex relationships and friendships in the play. Amber and Ruby have a complex relationship with their parents, as they have been abused by Harbans, but also feel blame themselves for not being able to protect Surinder from this. Ruby lashes out at Amber and calls her selfish for focusing on her running and school life and not helping her mum more, but this is perhaps due to her own resentment for not being able to make her own life choices. Amber still tries to love her father despite his actions, and believes him when he says he has changed, though Surinder is more suspicious of this.

Ruby and Jas' relationship has developed into a friendship, and Jas loves Ruby, but Ruby is still resentful that the marriage wasn't her choice. Jas is kind and loving and is willing to give Ruby the time she needs to decide if their relationship is what she wants.

Amber can't tell Tara and David the truth about her life, which causes tension in their friendship, as they can't always understand her actions, and don't know what she is going through, so can't support her with this. Tara and David are shocked at how Amber treats Gemma, and both tell her this is unacceptable behaviour. Amber's bullying of Gemma is a way of lashing out and deflecting the anger, pain and fear she feels about her home life. Amber starts to deal with these feelings after escaping Harbans.

Beena helps Surinder to realise she can leave Harbans, and through teaching her to read, Amber and Ruby help her to realise she can live independently without him. Harbans has belittled and abused Surinder over the years to make her think she is worthless and useless, and by not allowing her to learn English, has prevented her from leading her own life fully.

The Man serves as a metaphor for the control Harbans had over his daughters; he invented the story to instil fear in both of them, and to control their behaviour. When they understand the story of the Man was made up, Amber and Ruby both feel lighter and free, as the fear of this happening to them has been lifted.

- What is different about David's relationship with Beena, and Amber's relationship with her parents?

- Why does Amber not tell David and Tara what is happening at home?

- If you were Ruby, how would you feel about Amber's talent in running?

- In your opinion, why does Amber attack Gemma?

- What do you think will happen to Ruby and Jas in the future?

Deprivation

Palm Wood Estate.
One of the roughest and biggest estates in the country.
Streets-in-the-sky dreams
turned to sinkhole nightmares.
A bunch of concrete towers,
looming over you.

Amber and her family live in deprivation. Surinder works long
hours for a low wage, and Harbans doesn't work. They receive
benefits but struggle to survive on these. Harbans and Surinder's
ability to work and earn an income are limited due to their lack
of English skills.

Deprivation is different to poverty: 'Deprivation consists of
more than just poverty. Poverty is not having enough money to
get by, whereas deprivation refers to a general lack of resources
and opportunities.' (data.southampton.gov.uk/economy/
deprivation-poverty)

The NHS explains that the factors that influence the index of
multiple deprivation are:

- Income

- Employment

- Education

- Health

- Crime

- Barriers to housing and services

- Living environment
  (england.nhs.uk/about/equality/equality-hub/national-
  healthcare-inequalities-improvement-programme/what-
  are-healthcare-inequalities/deprivation)

Amber describes her estate as 'rough'. In the play she doesn't have the same opportunities as Tara and David who have been on foreign holidays. Miss Sutton buys Amber some new trainers after hers rip, but it is suggested that Miss Sutton doesn't really understand Amber's situation, and what is holding her back from running. As Amber says, 'That's the problem with privilege. If you have it, it can be hard to imagine why others can't live as freely as you.'

Intersectionality is the term used to describe when multiple factors overlap in an issue, such as deprivation. For example, the Covid-19 pandemic highlighted that, in the UK, people from the Global Majority were more likely to test positive, fall severely ill and die. This is called health inequality, and there are many factors that influence this such as poverty, ethnicity, gender and disability.

There is also a connection between alcohol misuse and deprivation. Although studies have found that there are higher levels of non-drinkers in deprived areas, because of the cost factor of alcohol, there are also higher numbers of heavy drinkers. Furthermore, 'poorer people were still more likely to suffer alcohol harms.' There are lots of reasons for this, including lack of access to preventative services, and general poorer health, all linked to the multiple factors of deprivation. (alcoholchange.org.uk/policy/policy-insights/alcohol-and-inequalities)

- How can the UK tackle its levels of deprivation?

- What are the different things that Amber and her family are deprived of?

- Was Miss Sutton right to buy Amber some new trainers?

- Why is it hard to break the cycle of deprivation?

- How does deprivation affect a young person's experience of education in school?

Bullying

Rich mum and dad,
little Miss Perfect.
Acts all shy,
victim-like –
couldn't be
further from the truth.

AMBER. You really do think you're better than everyone else
don't you. […] You should be scared of me.

Bullying can happen in person or online, to children or adults.
It isn't just something that happens in the school playground, it
can happen in the workplace or the home. Bullying can include
making hurtful comments, baiting or taunting, physical hitting
or fighting, talking behind other people's backs, spreading
rumours or online bullying.

Bullies might not realise why they bully, or how bad they can
make other people feel. Some of the reasons people bully others
could be:

- They have problems at home or have experienced trauma
  or abuse.

- They are jealous of others.

- They are insecure.

- They are baited to bully others by another person.

- They may think that bullying makes them look 'cool' or
  'hard'.
  (bullybusters.org.uk/kids/why_do_people_bully)

- Why does Amber target Gemma in particular?

- Why do you think Amber is a bully?

- How do you think it makes Amber feel when she attacks Gemma?

- Should Tara and David have tried to understand Amber's actions more?

- How do you think Amber's school should respond to her bullying actions?

- Why does Harbans bully Beena in the street?

Activities

The following activities can be used to introduce students to the themes and narrative of *Run, Rebel* before or after reading the play. You could pick and choose from these activities or put them together for a longer workshop.

Content warning: The themes and synopsis contain detailed information about abuse which may be triggering. Please ensure this is appropriate for your group before sharing.

Exploring the Themes: Put students into groups and give each group one of the themes of the play. Ask students to read the information, to research their theme and to present back to the rest of the class. This could be done as a flip-learning task, where students take away the theme and research it as homework before coming back and presenting it in class.

Understanding the Synopsis: Put students into groups and give each group a copy of the full synopsis. Ask students to read the synopsis aloud, taking turns in reading to develop oracy. Then ask students to break down the synopsis into ten to fifteen key moments, and to write these on to a large piece of paper. This helps students to digest the synopsis and simplifies it for younger learners.

Still Images: Using the key moments from the synopsis, ask students to create ten to fifteen still images of each key moment. Encourage them to use levels, space, physical contact and to consider their body language and facial expressions. The images could be performed to music to create an emotive piece of physical theatre.

Collective Character: Put students into groups of three and give out Extract 1 from the script extracts which follow. Ask them to read, rehearse and perform the extract collectively in role as Amber. They can divide the lines up between them or speak in chorus, or a mixture of both. Words can be repeated, stressed, shouted, whispered, rapped, sung – encourage students to be creative in response to the text and play around with it. Encourage students to consider how they can creatively use space or physical movement to show Amber running in this scene.

Parallel Scenes: Put students into groups of four and give them Extract 2 from the script extracts. Ask them to stage this scene, considering how they will block and stage the parallel settings and mirrored dialogue. They could use cross-cutting or split-screen techniques, or could be more creative and abstract with the staging.

Thought Tracking: Using the exercise above, add two more students into each group, and ask them to stop the action at particular points and thought-track the characters. Thought-tracking means speaking the thoughts, rather than the lines of the characters. Consider what Gemma or Beena are thinking whilst they are being attacked, or what Amber or Harbans are thinking whilst they are attacking.

Script Extracts

Extract 1

No matter how small or quiet
I'm expected to be at home,
I find my voice on the running track
It's where I'm truly alive.
Words boomerang from trainer to tarmac,
creating ripples in every corner of my body
until all knock-downs, run-ins, face-offs and scraps
have been twisted, wrung, exhausted and
released up, up, up,
into the clouds and sky above.

I shift my thoughts
try and make sense of stuff
and come out the other side newer, happier, better.
ALWAYS better than before.
It feels like the world slows down.
Allowing me to catch up with thoughts that usually race.
I go to places in my head that aren't here,
of this place,
of this time.
The lines in my head get tangled see
running makes the lines straighter
turns down the rage in my stomach
loosens the phantom grip on my throat.
Running gives me a purpose.
Running,
gives me a reason to live.

Extract 2

TARA, DAVID, AMBER *and* GEMMA *at school.*
HARBANS *and* BEENA *in town.*

HARBANS. Oi. You! /

BEENA. Excuse me? /

AMBER. Oi! Gemma! /

TARA. Just leave it, Amber. /

DAVID. Just let it go, Amber.

HARBANS. You stay away from my wife and daughter, do you hear me? /

AMBER. I warned you, Gemma /

BEENA. You're Amber's dad? /

AMBER. You're a fat, ugly cow you know that? /

HARBANS. You know who I am, don't act dumb. I'm warning you /

AMBER. No amount of make-up can fix this whole situation. /

BEENA. Warning me? /

AMBER. What's the matter, Gemma? Cat got your tongue. /

DAVID. Come on, Ambs, leave her alone.

HARBANS. Yes. Stay out of my family's business.

BEENA. I'm not scared of you /

AMBER. You really do think you're better than everyone else, don't you. /

HARBANS. You should be scared of me /

AMBER. You should be scared of me. /

BEENA *walks away, strong but shaken.*

Extract 3

I'm not okay, He's going to come after us.

JAS. Who?

AMBER. The Man.

JAS. What man?

RUBY. Mr Garcha, who lives across the road. The one who murdered his daughter…

AMBER. Dad… Dad… always said… Always said… that he'd come for us if we ever… if we ever…

JAS. Mr Garcha at number forty-two?

RUBY. Yes.

JAS. He wouldn't hurt a fly.

SURINDER. That man is evil, people aren't always what they seem.

JAS. I've known him my whole life. I went to school with his daughters.

Both alive, both doing very well for themselves.

AMBER. How come we don't see the older one? She ran away and Mr Garcha found her and murdered her.

JAS. What? No, she's just moved away, trust me I'm friends with her. I can't believe what you've been told.

The three women sit in silence. Shocked.

SURINDER. All this time.

Beat.

AMBER (*to audience*). Something is changing.

SURINDER (*to audience*). Something is shifting.

RUBY (*to audience*). A weight has been lifted

MR GARCHA *waves at them. They wave back.*

A wish

SURINDER (*to audience*). I didn't know I had made

AMBER (*to audience*). Has been granted.